SULLIVAN
AND HIS
SATELLITES

SULLIVAN
AND HIS
SATELLITES

A SURVEY OF ENGLISH OPERETTAS
1860-1914

ALAN HYMAN

CHAPPELL AND COMPANY|ELM TREE BOOKS

Chappell & Company Limited
50 New Bond Street, London, W1A 2BR

London Amsterdam Brussels Hamburg
Johannesburg Madrid Milan Paris
Stockholm Sydney Toronto Wellington
Zurich New York

in association with
Elm Tree Books Ltd.,
90 Great Russell Street, London WC1B 3PT

First Published 1978
© Alan Hyman 1978

Designed by Ron Jones

Design and production in association with
Book Production Consultants,
7 Brooklands Ave, Cambridge.

Printed in Great Britain by
Symphony Reproductions
60-70 Roden St., Ilford, Essex. IG1 2AQ
A Polygram Company

Printed in Great Britain by

Phototypesetting by Print Origination,
Bootle, Merseyside L20 6NS

ISBN 0 903443 24 4

For
everyone who enjoys the
Gilbert and Sullivan operas
and who remembers
the music of
Merrie England

Contents

List of Illustrations ix

Foreword xi

Acknowledgements xv

Part 1 Gilbert and Sullivan in Orbit

    1 The German Reed nursery 3
    2 The gods get the bird 13
    3 The man of action 20
    4 *Pinafore* mania 29

Part 2 The Savoy triumvirate

    5 Monarchs of the Savoy 41
    6 Make way for *The Mikado* 52
    7 Gaiety George 65

Part 3 The Guv'nor calls the tune

    8 *Dorothy* upsets the applecart 77
    9 The fatal quarrel 86
   10 End of a golden era 107
   11 The peacock and the gentleman 117
   12 The Orpheus of Daly's 128

Part 4 Sullivan's mantle

   13 The hermit of Maida Vale 151
   14 The *Floradora* man 169
   15 Two of the best 181

Epilogue: Fortunes of war 201

Bibliography 215

Gilbert and Sullivan's Comic Operettas 217

Index of Operettas 218

General Index 220

By the same author:
The Rise and Fall of Horatio Bottomley
The Gaiety Years

List of Illustrations

1. Poster of *Ages Ago*   (Enthoven Collection, Victoria and Albert Museum)
2. *Trial by Jury*   (Mansell Collection)
3. Richard D'Oyly Carte   (Bridget D'Oyly Carte)
4. Sir William Gilbert   (Bridget D'Oyly Carte)
5. Sir Arthur Sullivan   (Bridget D'Oyly Carte)
6. George Grossmith and Jessie Bond in *H.M.S. Pinafore*   (Enthoven Collection, Victoria and Albert Museum)
7. Walter Passmore and Henry Lytton in *Patience*   (Enthoven Collection, Victoria and Albert Museum)
8. Rutland Barrington in *The Mikado*   (Radio Times Hulton Picture Library)
9. Caricature of George Grossmith in *Iolanthe*   (Mansell Collection)
10. George Edwardes   (Radio Times Hulton Picture Library)
11. Alfred Cellier   (Mander and Mitchenson Theatre Collection)
12. Rutland Barrington and Jessie Bond in *Ruddigore*   (Mander and Mitchenson Theatre Collection)
13. Rosina Brandram in *The Gondoliers*   (Enthoven Collection, Victoria and Albert Museum)
14. Exterior, Royal English Opera House   (Mansell Collection)
15. Edward Solomon   (Radio Times Hulton Picture Library)
16. Adrian Ross   (Lady Rosamund Trelawney)
17. Ivan Caryll   (Mander and Mitchenson Theatre Collection)
18. Lionel Monckton   (Mrs Dorothy Miskin)
19. Daly's with five favourite actresses   (Mander and Mitchenson Theatre Collection)
20. Sidney Jones   (Arthur Jones)
21. Daly's Orchestra tribute to Sidney Jones   (Arthur Jones)
22. Marie Tempest in *The Geisha*   (Radio Times Hulton Picture Library)
23. Letty Lind in *The Geisha*   (Mander and Mitchenson Theatre Collection)
24. Huntley Wright in *The Geisha* (Mander and Mitchenson Theatre Collection)
25. Sir Edward German   (Reginald Haines)
26. Cartoon of *Merrie England*   (Mander and Mitchenson Theatre Collection)
27. Percy Greenbank   (Miss Phyllis Greenbank)
28. Hayden Coffin and Ruth Vincent in *Tom Jones*   (Mander and Mitchenson Theatre Collection)
29. Leslie Stuart   (Drooglever and Co.)
30. Ada Reeve in *'Florodora'* (Mander and Mitchenson Theatre Collection)
31. Edna May in *The Belle of Mayfair*   (Mander and Mitchenson Theatre Collection)
32. Gertie Millar and Joe Coyne in *The Quaker Girl*   (Mander and Mitchenson Theatre Collection)

33. Howard Talbot   (Mrs Agnes Fidgeon)
34. Louie Frear in *A Chinese Honeymoon*   (Mander and Mitchenson Theatre Collection)
35. Scene from *The Arcadians*   (Enthoven Collection, Victoria and Albert)
36. Paul Rubens   (Radio Times Hulton Picture Library)
37. Isabel Jay and G.P. Huntley in *Miss Hook of Holland*   (Mander and Mitchenson Theatre Collection)
38. Phyllis Dare and George Grossmith, Jr. in *The Sunshine Girl*   (Mander and Mitchenson Theatre Collection)

Foreword

When Arthur Sullivan returned home from Leipzig Conservatoire in 1861 and was hailed as a musical prodigy, French music was all the rage in London theatres. It was over a decade before English composers developed their individual style; from then comic operas by Sullivan and operettas and musical comedies by other English composers dominated the light musical stage until the First World War. There is a theory that in order to write about Gilbert and Sullivan one ought to be a Savoyard in the sense of being an enthusiastic admirer of the Savoy operas; if there is anything in it, I can claim to be a Savoyard of long standing.

As a junior reporter on a London newspaper, I worried the life out of the News Editor till he agreed to let me cover Henry Lytton's last night at the Savoy when he played Ko-Ko in *The Mikado* and Jack Point in *The Yeomen of the Guard*. Before the war I worked on the film of *The Mikado* at Pinewood Studios; though it never won an Oscar, it taught me a great deal about the Gilbert and Sullivan tradition.

I discovered much more about W.S. Gilbert, Arthur Sullivan and the indispensable D'Oyly Carte when researching recently for *The Gaiety Years,* and much regretted being forced to condense them into a single chapter because my subject was George Edwardes, who had once been Carte's right hand man. It is, therefore, a pleasure for me to take this opportunity of presenting my version of the great partnership of Gilbert and Sullivan.

However, I must make it clear that in surveying English operettas, I have made no attempt at a critical assessment of their music. There have already been some excellent books about the Gilbert and Sullivan operas, but in any case I am not a musicologist. My plan has been to concentrate on the people who created the operettas – the composers, librettists and lyric writers, the actors and actresses, and the leading impresarios of the period. But I could never have hoped to succeed in this project without the co-operation of some of the descendants of the composers at the very least. Incidentally, apart from Herbert Scott's biography of Edward German, very little is known about Sullivan's rivals and successors, such as Alfred Cellier, Edward Solomon, Ivan Caryll, Lionel Monckton, Sidney Jones, Leslie Stuart, Howard Talbot and Paul Rubens. I should like to thank all the descendants I have managed to trace for their kindness in assisting me to recover so many interesting facts from the past.

I am extremely grateful to Mrs Winifred German, a niece of Sir Edward German, for putting many of his papers at my disposal and inviting my wife and me to stay with her while I ploughed through the German collection.

Arthur Jones and his sister, Dorothy, gave me useful information about their father, Sidney Jones, composer of *The Geisha*. I thank them for this and for loaning me material relating to Sidney Jones.

I am grateful to Mrs Dorothy Miskin for reminiscences of her uncle, Lionel Monckton, an outstanding composer of operettas in addition to Gaiety musical comedies.

I am also grateful to Peter Cellier, great nephew of Alfred Cellier, for the loan of musical scores and documents about the composer whose comic opera, *Dorothy,* ran longer than *The Mikado.*

I have to thank the four daughters of Howard Talbot, joint composer of *The Arcadians,* for permission to quote from his papers in the Enthoven Collection at the Victoria and Albert Museum. Mrs Joy Ross made several corrections to my typescript which have been incorporated in the book.

I also thank the granddaughter of Leslie Stuart and Manchester Public Library for sending me fresh material about Stuart, who composed *Florodora* as well as popular songs like *Lily of Laguna* and *Soldiers of the Queen.*

I am much indebted to John George, a great grandson of George Grossmith, the first star of the Savoy operas. John George, who is a specialist on the musical pieces of this period, played me his splendid collection of records and tapes of operettas – a very stimulating experience.

The doyen of the lyric writers after Gilbert was Adrian Ross. I am most grateful to his daughters, Rosamund and Patience, for telling me a great deal about their illustrious parent, a Fellow of King's College, Cambridge, who became the Gaiety's leading lyricist almost by accident.

Lastly, I thank Phyllis Greenbank from the bottom of my heart, not only for valuable information about her father, Percy Greenbank, another outstanding lyric writer, but also for going to the trouble of reading some of my proofs. Miss Greenbank grew up in the ambience of Daly's Theatre; Percy and his brother, Harry, wrote many of the lyrics of the operettas produced there, and Phyllis Greenbank started out as a typist at Daly's aged sixteen and ended up as secretary to Cecil Paget, the general manager.

The difference between operetta and musical comedy is sometimes a very subtle one and can lead to controversy. In the case of English operettas, one can say that Gilbert and Sullivan's comic operas stand alone because their libretti and music are so beautifully integrated that almost every number in each piece makes a contribution towards the development of the story. The light operettas produced after *The Gondoliers* in the 'nineties by George Edwardes, Robert Courtneidge, Frank Curzon and others were, of course, not as 'pure' as the Savoy operas; the comedians were often allowed to gag instead of sticking to the script, and sometimes additional numbers were interpolated which had no bearing on the piece. However, the scores by Sidney Jones, Lionel Monckton, Paul Rubens and others rose to the standard of operetta.

Musical comedies, pioneered by George Edwardes, were a mixture of 'opera-bouffe', Gilbert and Sullivan, and the Gaiety burlesque. They had a slight romantic plot – the hero and heroine being singled out from the start – and after a few misunderstandings the girl always ended up in her lover's arms. There were colourful scenes, plenty of song-and-dance numbers, and – most important of all – a chorus of gorgeous girls who generally came on in the latest fashions. The comedians had the run of the stage and could gag away to their heart's content, often regaling the audience with topical jokes which had nothing whatsoever to do with the story.

Although this book is about operettas, it is almost inevitable that some of the best known musical comedies of the period have been included. I sincerely hope that my approximate definitions will help readers to sort out the two kinds of musical plays from each other. I have tried to keep to a chronological order, but this is not always possible, particularly when one builds a chapter round a composer like Sidney Jones or Edward German or narrates the success of Edwardes's musical plays in parallel with the declining fortunes of D'Oyly Carte's comic operas at the Savoy after the quarrel between Gilbert and Sullivan.

Acknowledgements

In writing this book I have, of course, been involved in a great deal of research in libraries. I would like to acknowledge all the help and unfailing courtesy I have received from the staff of the British Library at Bloomsbury, the Newspaper Library at Colindale, the London Library and the Music Section of the Westminster Public Library in Buckingham Palace Road.

As well as individuals mentioned in the Foreword, I am grateful to the following for permission to quote copyright material:

Reginald Alleen, *The First Night Gilbert and Sullivan*, Chappell, pages 21, 29, 33, 44, 48, 61, 135; William Archer, *Real Conversations*, Heinemann, page 142; Leslie Ayre, *The Gilbert and Sullivan Companion*, W. H. Allen, page 34; Leslie Baily, *The Gilbert and Sullivan Book*, Cassell, pages 7, 30, 53, 54, 57, 70, 71, 80, 81, 88, 92, 116; and *Gilbert and Sullivan and their World*, Thames and Hudson, pages 8, 9, 10, 24, 93; George Bancroft, *Stage and Bar*, Faber, page 42; Hector Bolitho, *Marie Tempest* Cobden Sanderson, page 127; Jessie Bond, *Reminiscences*, John Lane, pages 52, 58, 82; William Boosey, *"Fifty Years of Music"*, Ernest Benn, pages 120, 147, 204; J.B. Booth, *"London Town"*, Werner Laurie, page 198; Francois Cellier and Cunningham Bridgeman, *Gilbert, Sullivan and D'Oyly Carte*, Pitman page 104; Robert Courtneidge, *I was an Actor Once*, Hutchinson, pages 163, 193; Frances Donaldson, *Freddy Lonsdale*, page 199; Herman Finck, *My Melodious Memories*, Hutchinson, page 212; James Glover, *Jimmy Glover—His Book*, Methuen, pages 42, 110; George Grossmith, senior, *A Society Clown*, Arrowsmith, pages 25, 103; Sir Seymour Hicks, *25 Years of an Actor's Life*, Alston Rivers, page 58; John Hollingshead, *Gaiety Chronicles*, Constable, pages 13, 35, 36; Gervase Hughes, *Composers of Operettas*, Macmillan, pages 117, 128, 170; Alan Hyman, *"The Gaiety Years"*, Cassell, pages 36, 54; James Jupp, *The Gaiety Stage Door*, Cape, pages 177, 197; R.C. Lehmann, *Memories of Half a Century*, Smith Elder, page 11; Anita Leslie, *The Fabulous Mr. Jerome*, Hutchinson, pages 23, 24; Hesketh Pearson, *Gilbert and Sullivan*, Hamish Hamilton, pages 6, 28, 82, 100, 147; and *Gilbert, His Life and Strife*, Methuen, pages 54, 85, 90, 92, 96,

97, 98, 101, 102, 103, 104, 111, 112, 142; W. Macqueen Pope, *"Gaiety, Theatre of Enchantment"* W.H. Allen, page 127; and *The Melody Lingers On,* W.H. Allen, page 213; Ada Reeve, *Take it for a Fact,* Heinemann, pages 144, 191; Mrs. Margaret Clement Scott, *Old Days in Bohemian London,* London, page 54; William Herbert Scott, *Edward German,* Cecil Palmer, pages 152, 153, 154, 164, 165, 210, 211, 212; Jane Stedman, *Gilbert before Sullivan,* Routledge, pages 3, 4, 5, 11, 17, 18; Herbert Sullivan and Newman Flower, *Sir Arthur Sullivan,* Cassell, pages 14, 18, 35, 36, 48, 55, 56, 71, 81, 82, 84, 85, 93, 95, 102, 111, 112, 113, 134, 145, 146, 147; Ellaline Terriss, *Just a Little Bit of String,* Hutchinson, pages 120, 204; D. Forbes Winslow, *Daly's,* W.H. Allen, pages 128, 144, 162; P.G. Wodehouse and Guy Bolton, *Bring on the Girls,* Herbert Jenkins, page 205; Percy M. Young, *Sir Arthur Sullivan,* W. Norton and Co. New York, pages 7, 10, 19, 47, 49, 146.

I also wish to thank Bridget D'Oyly Carte Ltd. for permission to quote W.S. Gilbert's lyrics and am most grateful to Messrs Chappell and Co., and Ascherberg, Hopwood and Crew for their permission to quote lyrics from the following shows:
An Artist's Model, The Geisha, A Country Girl, Merrie England, The Quaker Girl, Miss Hook of Holland, The Arcadians and *The Sunshine Girl.* And I also thank Keith Prowse for permission to quote lyrics from *San Toy* and Stainer and Bell for permission to quote a lyric from *In Town.*

A word of thanks to Raymond Mander and Joe Mitchenson, whose work as theatre historians needs no introduction from me. Besides providing many illustrations from their unique collection at Sydenham, they have given me much expert advice. Professor Jane W. Stedman of Roosevelt University, Chicago richly deserves my thanks for extra information about W.S. Gilbert and calling my attention to another chapter in the life of that highly immoral Victorian composer, Edward Solomon, also for her kindness in checking all the proofs relating to Gilbert and Sullivan. A final word of thanks to Mrs Pat Baer, who has typed this manuscript from an early stage and never complained about the number of alterations in my horrible handwriting which she has managed to decipher. I have tried to keep to a chronological order, but this is not always possible, particularly when one builds a chapter round a composer like Sidney Jones or Edward German or narrates the success of Edwardes's musical plays in parallel with the declining fortunes of D'Oyly Carte's comic operas at the Savoy after the quarrel between Gilbert and Sullivan.

Steyning, 1977

PART 1
Gilbert and Sullivan in Orbit

CHAPTER ONE

THE GERMAN REED NURSERY

Gilbert and Sullivan opera was born among the Reeds.

W.S. GILBERT

In the unlikely event that a playgoer possessed a time machine and could transport himself back to London in the 1850s, he would have found French music in almost every theatre. When he went out for an evening of light music he would probably have had to choose between a French operetta specially adapted into English so that the sexual motif had been watered down to a mere innuendo, or a burlesque piece loosely based on a legend or a famous story, and invariably accompanied by the music of a French light composer. One has to thank Mr and Mrs German Reed, both of whom had grown up in the theatre, for giving English composers the opportunity of creating their individual style of comic opera.

Mrs German Reed had been Priscilla Horton, a talented actress who had made her name playing Ariel in *The Tempest*. Dark, handsome, genial and lively, Priscilla Horton was an excellent mimic and had a fine contralto voice. While appearing at the Haymarket Theatre, she fell in love with the conductor of the orchestra, Thomas German Reed, and married him in 1844. German Reed, a versatile musician, could play every instrument in the band; he could adapt Continental pieces into English and arrange them and was also a competent composer. In addition to this, he was a useful comedian who had started his career as a concert entertainer.

The German Reeds started their first stage performances at St Martin's Hall in 1854 but, to overcome the great Victorian prejudice against theatres, they advertised their productions euphemistically as 'Illustrative Gatherings'. Their venture prospered and they moved to larger premises at the Gallery of Illustration, a bijou theatre with a

3

good view from every seat at 14 Regent Street, Waterloo Place. Their seats cost from one to five shillings, which was cheaper than the other playhouses, and their entertainments were described in such innocent language that even clergymen and maiden aunts could visit them with a clear conscience; plays were called 'illustrations', the roles in them were 'assumptions', and audiences were still called 'gatherings'. The German Reeds produced musical pieces with small casts; there was no chorus, very little scenery, and a simple accompaniment on a piano and a harmonium. The general impression was that the Gallery of Illustration provided its patrons with musical entertainment of an almost religious character. Its audiences of clergymen, schoolmasters, doctors and middle class families in all walks of life were made to feel that at the Gallery they were in a much more refined atmosphere than in any other theatre in London. F.C. Burnand, who wrote several pieces for the German Reeds, said that whenever you visited the Gallery 'you felt that you were attending a meeting . . . and that the attendants were somehow not very distantly related to pew-openers, or they might have been pew-openers themselves, only slightly disguised' At first the German Reeds produced farces based on the mistaken identity joke, their success depending on the skill with which the artistes could carry off two or three roles in a piece. The company was led by Priscilla Horton (Mrs German Reed) and John Parry. By the mid-sixties the Gallery of Illustration had become a favourite attraction; one newspaper called it 'incomparably the best entertainment house in London.'

Then Thomas German Reed grew more ambitious. In 1867 he took a lease of St George's Hall in Upper Regent Street, a bigger theatre than the Gallery, and engaged a chorus and a first rate orchestra of forty for a season which included a revival of *The Beggars' Opera*. His first presentation at St George's Hall was *La Contrabandista*, a comic opera by F.C. Burnand and Arthur Sullivan. The latter, although he was only twenty-five, was regarded as the white hope of English music on the strength of his incidental music for *The Tempest*, his Irish symphony and his oratorios. It was unfortunate that *La Contrabandista* had an involved and rather tedious libretto which defeated Sullivan's score, and the piece came off

4

after a few weeks.

But on March 29, 1869, the German Reeds presented *Cox and Box*, a short comic opera by Sullivan and Burnand, at the Gallery of Illustration; this three-handed farce ran for 300 performances and was the biggest success the German Reeds had ever had. It is the story of two men who occupy the same room in a boarding house, but don't realize it because Cox works in the daytime and Box works at night. Their rascally landlord, Sergeant Bouncer, nearly gets caught out once or twice, but whenever he's in a tight corner he sings, 'Rataplan, rataplan, I'm a military man.' However, Cox unexpectedly gets a holiday one day and comes home to find Box in his room. They discover they are both involved with the same unattractive girl, and at the end of the piece they are suddenly convinced they are long-lost brothers. Sullivan's score squeezed every jot of humour out of the farce. The *Daily Telegraph* praised him 'for linking exquisite melodies to idiotic words'. For instance, in one scene Cox takes Box's mutton chop off the stove and substitutes his bacon, and croons, 'Hushabye, bacon, on the coal top.'

On the same bill as *Cox and Box* there had been a short piece entitled *No Cards* by W.S. Gilbert, already well known as a humourous writer and a promising playwright; German Reed had written the music for it. This operetta had four characters, who all assume various disguises in the course of a tale about Mr Churchmouse, a poor man who determines to marry the girl he loves despite competition from wealthy Mr. L.S.D. It turns out that she is an heiress which leads to a happy ending. Mrs Priscilla Reed had a splendid part which gave her several changes of roles during the piece. Arthur Cecil, a very gentlemanly actor, made a great hit in the part of Mr Churchmouse. *No Cards* had a limited appeal and only ran a short time.

However, in November the German Reeds presented *Ages Ago*, another piece by Gilbert, with music by Fred Clay, an accomplished composer who was Sullivan's best friend. Clay invited Sullivan to come and watch a rehearsal of *Ages Ago*. Arthur Sullivan was dark, rather short and stout, and was immaculately dressed in a frock coat. His olive complexion was inherited from his Italian mother and he had bright, luminous eyes. Clay introduced him to W.S. Gilbert, a

5

handsome, fair-haired man with blue eyes. Over six foot, he had a military bearing and great self assurance. Six years older than Sullivan, he seemed to tower over the composer. Without a moment's hesitation, Gilbert rapped out:

> You will be able to decide a question for me, Mr Sullivan. I maintain that a composer can express a musical theme perfectly upon the simple tetrachord of Mercury, in which there are no diatonic intervals at all, as upon the much more complicated diapason ... which embraces in its perfect consonance all the single, double and inverted chords.

As a matter of fact, Gilbert knew very little about music and was pulling Sullivan's leg, and also practising the effect of a speech he was writing for a pretentious music critic; he had cribbed the whole thing from an article on 'Harmony' in the Encyclopedia Britannica. Sullivan realized what Gilbert was up to and politely asked him to repeat the question. After Gilbert had done so, he promised to think the matter over for a few days. But, of course, the question never did get answered.

Arthur Seymour Sullivan, the second son of Thomas Sullivan, a struggling Irish musician, had been born at Boscobel Terrace, Lambeth, on May 13, 1842. Later on, Thomas Sullivan became bandmaster at the Royal Military College, Sandhurst, which helped the family finances considerably. His Italian wife had been Maria Coughlan and was half Jewish through her mother, a Righi. The fact that Arthur Sullivan was partly Jewish helps to explain why he was so passionately devoted to his family throughout his life. He was a musical prodigy: at eight he had mastered all the instruments in his father's band and could play flute, clarinet, horn, cornet, trombone and euphonium. His beautiful singing voice won him a place in the Chapel Royal choir; he had to live away from home and came under the strict rule of the Reverend Thomas Helmore in Chelsea.

Arthur Sullivan went on to the Royal Academy of Music where he showed extraordinary talent for his age and composed several short pieces. At sixteen he won the coveted Mendelssohn Scholarship, which entitled him to free tutition at Leipzig Conservatoire for two years. No doubt his stay in Germany played a vital part in

Sullivan's musical development; it was immensly stimulating to leave 'philistine' England for a country where music was part of the daily life of the people and he was able to meet great composers like Robert Schumann and Franz Liszt. Sullivan already had a knack for getting on with people who could help him in his career. Clara Barnett, his friend and fellow student at the Conservatoire, wrote years later about Sullivan:

It was part of his nature to ingratiate himself with everyone that crossed his path. He always wanted to make an impression and, what is more, he always succeeded in doing it . . . In that way he got into personal touch with most of the celebrities . . . He was a natural courtier, which did not prevent him, however, from being a very lovable person.

Sullivan returned to England in 1861, having already been praised in Leipzig for his incidental music for *The Tempest*. He soon made the acquaintance of George Grove, the influential Secretary of the Crystal Palace, then a leading musical centre. The following year his revised Tempest music was played privately and Grove accepted it for performance at the Crystal Palace. The work had a resounding success when first played on April 5, 1862. Sullivan, who was only nineteen, woke up next morning to find himself famous. On the Continent England was known as 'the land without music'; Sullivan resolved to do everything in his power to advance the cause of English music. His services were soon in demand to conduct at music festivals up and down the country. He composed some serious music and was accepted as part of the musical establishment, his charming personality making him a popular figure. Society opened its doors to the personable young composer and, just as Offenbach had conquered the salons of Paris, Sullivan soon became the darling of the London drawing rooms.

He composed under the strong influence of Mendelssohn, which makes it understandable that Queen Victoria and Prince Albert put him on a very high pedestal. When Edward, Prince of Wales married Princes Alexandra, the Queen asked Sullivan to write a Te Deum in their honour; it was so well liked that he became the unofficial Composer Laureate and Master of the Queen's Music for the rest of his life. This marked the begining of his friendship with the Prince of

Wales and with his brother, the Duke of Edinburgh. The Prince of Wales found Sullivan a most agreeable companion; he became a regular guest at Marlborough House and was sometimes invited to stay at Sandringham. The Duke of Edinburgh was a good amateur violinist; he and Sullivan became close friends, and the composer often played the piano accompaniment to his violin solos.

However, Sullivan earned very little from writing serious music and giving music lessons, so he took an appointment as organist and choir master at St Michael's Church, Chester Square, which brought him in a salary of £80 a year. He worked hard training the choir at St Michael's; there were plenty of sopranos in the district, but it was very difficult to find basses. He solved it by going to the local police station at Gerald Road and borrowing several bobbies with promising voices for his choir. During this period he wrote church music and popular ballads, which soon began to sell well.

George Grove, who had become one of Sullivan's closest friends, introduced him to the affluent Scott Russell family, who lived at Norwood. John Scott Russell, a distinguished engineer, had been an associate of Brunel's on the 'Great Eastern' project. Sullivan became a regular visitor to the house and used to delight in spending summer evenings in the scented garden at Norwood, discussing every subject under the sun with the clever people in the Scott Russell circle. The Scott Russell girls, Rachel and Louise, took a great liking to Arthur Sullivan; both of them were attractive and extremely musical. Rachel fell madly in love with Sullivan and he reciprocated her passion, although she was mercurial and would change from ecstasy to misery in a moment. When they quarrelled, Louise used to act as peacemaker. It is probable that Sullivan had an affair with Rachel; they certainly became unofficially engaged. He kept her letters to him all his life and treasured them. In 1866 she wrote: 'If you are ready to marry me next year well and good. I will tell Mama and Papa when you see the project close before you without a doubt – free of debt – and then there will be no reasonable objection.'

Although Sullivan earned very little he was extravagant and often got into debt. John Scott Russell had a poor opinion of him, regarding him as a penniless composer and an unsuitable match for his daughter. Rachel was passionately interested in Arthur Sullivan's music; when he was writing his Irish symphony she wrote:

Is the symphony in D getting on? Do write it, my bird. It is the language in which you talk to me. I also want you to write an octet. Mendelssohn's is splendid, and I am sure you could do a glorious thing. Will you?

A year afterwards she said:

I want you to write an opera – a grand, vigorous great work. Oh, strain every nerve for my sake... I want you to write something for which all the world must acknowledge your talent...

Towards the end of 1866 John Scott Russell decided that Sullivan was totally unworthy of Rachel; Sullivan was banned from the house and Rachel told not to see him any more. They had to meet secretly and their romance gradually petered out. Soon after the ban she wrote: 'If when you get this you want to see me dreadfully I will go to the rookery at half past 3.'

In October Thomas Sullivan died suddenly. Arthur adored his father and was beside himself with grief. 'My dear, dear Father, whom I loved so passionately and who returned my love a hundred-fold if that were possible', he wrote to Mrs R.C. Lehmann. 'Oh, it is so hard to think that I shall never see his dear face again. I am able to be strong for my dear mother's sake... but at night, when I am alone, then the wound breaks out, and I think of him and his tender love and care for me – and now he is gone for ever.'

His father's death inspired Sullivan to write *In Memoriam*, an oratorio for the Norwich Festival which was hailed as a masterpiece. He brought his mother to keep house for him at Claverton Street, Pimlico, which probably helped to hasten the end of his romance with Rachel Scott Russell. She wrote to him in a desperate tone the following year: 'Will you let me come and forget everything for six bright hours with you? Will you let me? ... I have never been happy for an hour since we parted in that little room [George Grove's office at the Crystal Palace] and I ache for a little happiness... There is always the sad yawning chasm and it gets bigger rather than smaller...'

Rachel decided before the year was out that it was hopeless for

1. The original poster of *Ages Ago* by W.S. Gilbert, produced by the German Reeds at the Gallery of Illustration, Regent Street, in 1869. It was the germ of the comic opera, *Ruddigore,* years later.

her and Arthur Sullivan to go on seeing each other any more, and wrote him this moving farewell letter:

> Your young life shall not be dimmed by the mention of a hope which will never be fulfilled. You have others to work for and your beautiful genius to live for, and neither I, nor any other woman on God's earth is worth wasting one's life for.

Rachel Scott Russell went out of his life forever, and it seems clear that none of the women he knew after her was able to inspire him in the same way to compose serious music. Three years later she married a tea planter and went to live abroad.

After Sullivan's first meeting with W.S. Gilbert at the Gallery of Illustration, the two men made no attempt to strike up a friendship, though they met sometimes at the homes of mutual friends. Gilbert's piece, *Ages Ago*, produced on November 22, 1869, was a great advance on his previous libretti. The *Daily Telegraph* thought it was 'the best yet at the popular little Gallery', and it ran for over 350 performances. It had an ingenious plot centring round Sir Ebenezer Fare, a nouveau riche merchant who buys Glen Cockaleekie Castle complete with portraits of family ancestors without a notion of the trouble he has let himself in for. The title deed turns up after a

10

hundred years, proving that his neice's poor suitor is the rightful owner of the castle. While everybody is sleeping, the family ancestors step out of their frames and there are terrible complications because a young male and a female ancestor fall in love with each other but she is fifteenth century and he is sixteenth century, so that she is old enough to be his mother. Gilbert, the first playwright who had ever made ghosts behave like human beings on the stage, obviously borrowed a great deal from *Ages Ago* when he came to write *Ruddigore*.

His next comic opera, *Our Island Home*, was produced at the Gallery on June 20, 1870. Set on an island in the Indian Ocean, it had been specially written for the four resident stars of the theatre, Mr and Mrs German Reed, Arthur Cecil and Fanny Holland. They all appeared under their own names, but Gilbert totally changed their characters; gentle-natured Arthur Cecil became a deep-dyed villain, while genial Priscilla Reed was transformed into a domineering shrew. Gold is discovered on the island just as Captain Bang (played by Alfred Reed, the German Reeds' son) turns up. He is revealed as the long-lost son of the German Reeds, but there is a dreadful drawback: as he has taken the pirates' oath he is bound to do his duty and kill everybody on the island. They find out just in time that, as he is twenty one, he is released from his pirate duties; so it all ends happily.

Our Island Home was an advance on *Ages Ago* but it was not nearly as successful; the character of Captain Bang obviously inspired Fredric, the pirate orphan in *The Pirates of Penzance*. After that the Gallery presented an entertainment by Gilbert entitled *A Sensation Novel*, which is about a prolific author of romances whose characters come out of his pages and contradict the development of his plot at the end of each volume. (Pirandello used the same theme brilliantly in his play, *Six Characters in search of an Author* about fifty years later). Gilbert's fascinating outline of *A Sensation Novel* has recently come to light:

An author has entered into a compact with the Demon of Romance by which he is able to turn out 53 volumes per annum. The stock characters provided by the Demon include the virtuous governess, the unemployed young Sunday school teacher, the sensation detective, the wicked baronet, and the beautiful fiend with

11

yellow hair and the panther-like movement. They have wishes, schemes and plans of their own, but the fulfilment of them is for the time being in the hands of the Author, to whom they are entrusted. They have the power of coming to life at the end of the first and second volumes, and immediately before the last chapter of the third, to talk over the events that have taken place and to arrange plans for the future – plans which are too often frustrated by the Author's arbitrary will.

The virtuous governess, the heroine, can't bear the hero, the Sunday school teacher, considering him a milksop – but she finds the wicked baronet irresistible. On the other hand the Sunday school teacher adores the yellow-haired adventuress. *A Sensation Novel* was not a hit because the Gallery patrons thought it indelicate, particularly when the adventuress boasted that she had strangled the engine driver of an L.N.E.R. train, changed clothes with him, and driven the train on to Leeds.

Gilbert wrote two more pieces for the German Reeds, of which the better was *Happy Arcadia* for which Frederic Clay composed the score. Gilbert found that writing for the Gallery was like having a laboratory in which he could experiment on a small scale with all manner of ideas, and could rely on the German Reeds to give him adequate time in which to rehearse his pieces. It was typical of German Reed productions that the artistes paid special attention to every word of their songs to avoid the music drowning them – an innovation later adopted by Gilbert in his comic operas with Sullivan.

Sullivan's career as a composer of comic operas was also influenced by the German Reeds, for he tended to equate his work by the popular verdict on it. Thus the enormous success of *Cox and Box*, which he had only written at first for a charity performance, made him confident that he could write another comic opera if he set his mind to it. Since his first meeting with Gilbert, he had composed a number of ballads which had sold so well that Boosey, the music publishers, had agreed to pay him a retainer of £400 a year to write ballads for them on the most generous terms.

W.S. Gilbert and Arthur Sullivan collaborated for the first time on *Thespis or The Gods grow Old*, a comic opera presented at the Gaiety Theatre as a Christmas entertainment in 1871. Since *Thespis* marked the beginning of their great partnership, it deserves a chapter to itself.

CHAPTER TWO

THE GODS GET THE BIRD

We are disappointed when we find the applause but fitful, the laughter scarcely spontaneous, and the curtain falling not without sound of disapprobation.

CLEMENT SCOTT'S NOTICE OF THESPIS,
DAILY TELEGRAPH, DECEMBER 1871

The old Gaiety Theatre, which stood at the eastern end of the Strand opposite the church of St Mary-le-Strand, had been opened by John Hollingshead in 1868. 'Honest John', as he was called affectionately, was a self-made journalist who had once worked for Charles Dickens on 'Household Words' and had not become a theatre manager till he was forty. Hollingshead had catholic tastes: during his long period at the Gaiety he gave the public a variety of entertainment, ranging from Shakespeare and opera to pantomime and burlesque. The theatre was run in conjunction with the Gaiety restaurant next door, which caused Hollingshead to suggest putting up this notice over the door:

> John Hollingshead, licensed dealer in legs, short skirts, French adaptations, Shakespeare, Taste and the Musical Glasses.

His playhouse became renowned for its burlesque pieces, in which comedians spoke in rhyming doggerel, made outrageous puns and cracked topical jokes, while the chorus consisted of buxom females very scantily dressed in tights. W.S. Gilbert wrote a burlesque of 'Robert the Devil' for the opening night and there were two other items in the generous bill. But 'Robert the Devil' was unquestionably the success of the evening; Gilbert had worked well, but it owed a great deal to Nellie Farren, the leading lady, a clever actress, a marvellous male impersonator and a sprightly dancer. Before very long dynamic little Nellie Farren became the queen of the Gaiety and the idol of the gallery boys.

In the autumn of 1871 John Hollingshead asked Gilbert to write him a comic opera for Christmas and suggested that Arthur Sullivan should do the score. As Sullivan had recently turned down an offer from the German Reeds to collaborate with Gilbert, the latter thought it would be difficult to persuade him; it was a pleasant surprise when Sullivan accepted the commission. Gilbert wrote the libretto of *Thespis or The Gods grow Old* very quickly, but Sullivan did not finish setting it to music till December, only leaving them a week for rehearsals in order to produce the piece on Boxing Day.

Hollingshead decided to make *Thespis* a vehicle for Nellie Farren and J.L. Toole, the comedian, despite the fact that neither of his stars had much of a voice. Nellie Farren, who revelled in boys' roles, played the young god, Mercury, and J.L. Toole was cast as Thespis, leader of a troupe of strolling players. Neither of them could sing Sullivan's music adequately; in fact when the composer took the company through his music he complained: 'Few actors in the cast could sing, and of those who pretended to hardly any could be said to compass more than six notes.'

The theme of *Thespis* was that all the gods and goddesses on Mount Olympus have grown old and incapable of doing their proper work with the result that they make young Mercury the celestial drudge. Nellie Farren as Mercury sang this number about her plight:

Oh, I'm the celestial drudge,
From morning to night I must stop at it,
Oh errands all day I must trudge,
And I stick to my work till I drop at it!

In summer I get up at one,
(As a good-natured donkey I'm ranked for it)
Then I'll go and light up the Sun,
And Phoebus Apollo gets thanked for it!

Well, well, it's the way of the world,
And will be through all its futurity;
Though noodles are baroned and earled,
There's nothing for clever obscurity!

A band of strolling players climb up Mount Olympus for a picnic and meet Jupiter and the other gods. Jupiter makes a contract with

Thespis, the leader, for the actors to change places with the tired gods and to do their duties, but young Mercury will stay with them on Mount Olympus to show Thespis and the others their duties and make sure things are running smoothly. Thespis, a superior person, has an amusing number about a Chairman who came to grief through being too free-and-easy:

> I once knew a man who discharged a function
> On the North South East West Fiddlesex junction,
> He was conspicuous exceeding
> For his affable ways and his easy breeding.
> Although a Chairman of Directors,
> He was hand in glove with the ticket inspectors,
> He tipped the guards with brand-new fivers
> And sang little songs to the engine drivers.

When Thespis and the actors are left in charge at Mount Olympus they do everything wrong. Tipseon, for instance, makes all the vines yield ginger beer, but Mercury doesn't interfere with them for a year and then draws up a list of complaints. The gods return in a great rage because Thespis and his band have turned the earth upside down, and Jupiter sends the actors back to earth.

Thespis, a work of wit and imagination, was worth a dozen pantomimes or run-of-the-mill burlesques, but it needed better singers and it had been impossible to give it a worthy production with only a week to rehearse in. Gilbert had done his best to teach the artistes the appropriate style he required for his ironical, topsy-turvy comedy. He broke new ground by making the chorus part of the action; until then choristers used to stand about on the stage doing nothing until they had to sing a chorus.

There was a crowded house at the Gaiety for the premiere of *Thespis* on Boxing Day, December 26, 1871. But the gallery and the piltites, used to the doggerel verse and blatant innuendos of the burlesques, hadn't the foggiest idea who Jupiter or Mercury or Apollo were, so that all the allusions to Greek gods went right over their heads. The piece was badly received, the gallery and the pit actually booed it. There were frequent waits, and frequent indisposition to take up points marred the plesant effect of Mr Sullivan's music and destroyed the pungency of Mr Gilbert's humour.' said one of the critics.

But Clement Scott, the famous *Daily Telegraph* critic, greatly admired the piece: 'The story, written by Mr W.S. Gilbert in his liveliest manner, is so original, and the music contributed by Mr Arthur Sullivan so pretty and fascinating that we are ... disappointed when we find the applause but fitful, the laughter scarcely spontaneous, and the curtain falling not without sound of disapprobation ... The verdict of last night cannot be taken as final ... *Thespis* is too good to be put on one side and cold-shouldered in this fashion.'

The Standard wrote: 'Mr John Hollingshead ... has judiciously called on Mr W.S. Gilbert to furnish him with an original opera-extravaganza, and entrusted the musical setting to Mr Arthur Sullivan ... Mr Gilbert has happily provided the composer with everything he could desire ... The composer in return has wedded Mr Gilbert's verses to some exquisite music, has pleasingly coloured his scenes, and given character to some of his mythological personages ... Mr Sullivan has been very happy in infusing a certain amount of sentiment into several of the characters...'

However, *Thespis* never overcame the bad impression that had been created on the first night; it had a medium run and then Hollingshead took it off. Gilbert and Sullivan shook hands on the last night and walked away in different directions. It had been a very pleasant collaboration, and Sullivan had been most impressed by the skill Gilbert had shown in directing their piece in such a short space of time; but neither of them had any reason for supposing they would ever work together again.

The initials 'W.S.' in Gilbert's name stood for William Schwenck; he had been born in a house in Southampton Street, only a few yards away from the site of the Savoy Theatre. The son of a naval surgeon, he grew up in a unhappy middle class household; his parents had begun to quarrel when he was only a boy and they separated when he was nineteen. Gilbert, the only son, disliked his mother and wrote to her on several occasions complaining about her treatment of his

16

father. After being turned down by the Army at the end of the Crimean War, he started work as a clerk in the Education Department of the Privy Council and loathed every minute of his time there. Luckily, he inherited a small legacy and threw up the job and became a barrister in 1864. Though Gilbert never made a living at the Law, his experience in the Courts was invaluable to him when he came to write plays.

At first he wrote stories for weekly journals and often illustrated them under the signature of 'Bab', his nickname at home. H.J. Byron, the editor of *Fun*, the rival paper to *Punch*, liked his first contribution so much that he invited Gilbert to write comic ballads for *Fun* every week. A fellow contributor to *Fun* was Tom Robertson, the playwright, who had founded a natural school of drama when he wrote *Ours* for Marie Wilton and Squire Bancroft in 1865. Until then the theatres had been dominated by actors with a florid style of playing; even Barry Sullivan the Shakesperian star, was known as the prince of barnstormers. They acted their heads off and it was said that real life never got through the stage door. Tom Robertson, who produced his own plays, wrote about recognisable people in *Ours*, *Caste* and *Society*. His characters actually had a meal on the stage, which was such an innovation that his plays were called 'cup-and-saucer' comedies.

After Tom Robertson and Gilbert had become good friends, Gilbert was invited to come and watch his rehearsals. Years later Gilbert said that Robertson had invented stage management. He learnt a great deal from seeing Robertson rehearse the Bancroft company and give 'life and variety to the scene by breaking it up with all sorts of little incidents and delicate by-play'. Robertson aimed to eliminate the star system in favour of ensemble playing.

In 1867 Gilbert married Lucy Turner, the pretty, petite, fair-haired daughter of an Army officer; he was then thirty one, while Lucy was only seventeen. It turned out a happy marriage, although she had to put up with a husband who was an incorrigible flirt with a weakness for pretty women who were tall and fair. During his long career Gilbert flirted with many women, including several actresses, but there is no reason to suppose that he went to bed with any of them.

During 1871 Gilbert had six comedies produced in London, the outstanding one being *Pygmalion and Galatea,* presented by Mrs Madge Kendal and her husband, W.H. Kendal, at the Haymarket on December 9, 1871. Galatea proved an ideal role for Mrs Kendal, who was beautiful in addition to her great talents, and the piece ran for over 200 performances. Mary Anderson, the American actress, produced *Pygmalion and Galatea* in New York in 1881, and also played Galatea.

Gilbert's entertainment, *Happy Arcadia,* had been presented at the Gallery of Illustration in 1871. This cynical piece depicted the inhabitants of Arcadia getting so bored with their idyllic life that, when a necromancer appears, they are all delighted to change places. He leaves behind a magic ring, a cloak, a cap and a stick, each of which gives its holder a magic wish. Priscilla Reed gave a splendid performance as an Arcadian matron who changes into her daughter's suitor and proceeds to smoke a pipe. Nobody seemed to mind the transvestite motif, but the critics fell on Gilbert for daring to use a theme which implied that pure and innocent pleasure could be too insipid to bear.

Gilbert wrote his last piece for the German Reeds in 1875; but by then he and Arthur Sullivan had collaborated on *Trial by Jury,* a miniature masterpiece which was in advance of anything ever produced at the Gallery of Illustration. But working with the German Reeds had been an important stepping-stone in Gilbert's career. Priscilla and Thomas Reed had taught him that it was a paying proposition to write pieces that would never bring a blush to a maiden's cheek, and he never forgot the lesson.

After the failure of *Thespis* Sullivan returned to his serious music, driving himself so hard that he took no time off for a holiday. As England's leading composer, he was often asked to write oratorios and other musical works for the big festivals, in addition to which he was in great demand as a conductor at leading centres like Manchester, Birmingham, Leeds, Edinburgh, Norwich and Bournemouth. Sometimes he would spend the whole day composing, then catch the night train to Manchester or Birmingham in order to conduct the orchestra next day. Wherever he went, Sullivan took his little notebook with him and jotted down in it sketches for songs and fresh musical phrases. In 1872 he began to suffer from a kidney complaint; this weakness was to last for the rest of his life and cause him much pain and suffering. But although the doctors diagnosed that the trouble came from his kidneys, there is a recent theory that he really had an infection of the bladder.

At this period the London light musical stage was still flooded with the work of French composers. At the Gaiety the burlesques were generally accompanied by music adapted from Offenbach or one of his contemporaries. Offenbach was undoubtedly the most popular composer in England; playgoers had a choice of several of his opera-bouffes, notably *La Belle Helene, The Grand Duchess of Gerolstein,* and *La Périchole.* Charles Lecocq was represented by his masterpiece, *La Fille de Madame Angot; Le Petit Faust* by Hervé ran quite well; and Planquette's *Les Cloches de Corneville* was probably the biggest success of all.

One man who had seen *Thespis* agreed with Clement Scott that it was a delightful piece and had deserved a better fate. He was Richard D'Oyly Carte, a concert and lecture agent aged 27, a man of medium height with dark curly hair who wore a beard. He had shrewd eyes and spoke very little, but listened carefully to what everybody had to say. Very cultured and an excellent musician, he was also a sharp business man. Carte had composed operettas for the German Reeds, the best of them being *Happy Hampstead.* He had set up as a concert agent because he was intelligent enough to realize that he would find it hard going to make a living as a musician.

Carte's ambition was to become an impresario of musical plays and he believed that being a musician himself was bound to be an asset to him. John Hollingshead had had W.S. Gilbert and Arthur Sullivan under his management and let them go after *Thespis;* D'Oyly Carte had the flair to recognize that if the two collaborators had a sympathetic manager and were given adequate time to rehearse their pieces properly, they would write memorable comic operas in the future. But the vital factor in his calculations was that their ideal manager was Richard D'Oyly Carte.

CHAPTER THREE

THE MAN OF ACTION

Sullivan and I have the same sense of humour.
When I tell him a joke he understands it immediately.
I never have to tell it twice, which is fatal.

W.S. GILBERT

Richard D'Oyly Carte had become one of the leading concert agents in
London by 1875; his office at Craig's Court off Shaftsbury Avenue
seemed to be busy from morning to night. Carte had a flair for
summing up the men and women who came into his office in a
minute, and he rarely made a mistake about them. Perhaps the wisest
decision he ever took was to engage Helen Lenoir as his secretary.
This remarkable Scotswoman had thrown up a brilliant career, after
taking honours in four subjects at London University, to become an
actress. But, deciding she would never get to the top, she applied for a
job with D'Oyly Carte and got taken on at once. In a short time Helen
Lenoir had acquired an extraordinary grasp of the agency business,
and in the eventful years ahead she became invaluable to Carte.
Though he was diplomatic and had great vision, he was inclined to be
erratic. Helen Lenoir had her feet on the ground; she was very
pracitcal, had a wonderful head for figures and was a first-rate
negotiator.

One of Carte's clients, Madame Selina Dolaro, an opera singer of
the second rank, arranged to present a season of light operas at the
Royalty Theatre, Soho, and asked Carte to manage it. When she was
about to produce Offenbach's operetta, *La Périchole*, Carte advised
her it was too short for an evening's entertainment and undertook to
find her a curtain-raiser. Just at the right moment W.S. Gilbert called
at the Royalty to see Carte, who asked if he had a suitable piece.
Gilbert offered him *Trial by Jury*, which had originally appeared as an
illustrated ballad in *Fun*. Carl Rosa had been going to set it to music,
but the project had fallen through owing to the death of his wife,

Madame Parepa Rosa, the opera singer.

Trial by Jury, a witty and engaging send-up of the Law, appealed immensely to D'Oyly Carte. He promised there and then to put it on, but only on condition that the score should be written by Arthur Sullivan and not Carl Rosa. Carte's condition depressed Gilbert because he knew Sullivan had been working on serious music ever since the failure of *Thespis*. However, a few days later he called on Sullivan at his new flat at Queens Mansions, arriving in the middle of a snowstorm.

He read *Trial by Jury* to Arthur Sullivan in a mood of pessimism, as though he felt it was small beer and quite unworthy of an author whose comedies had been produced at the Haymarket. Sullivan's diary takes up the story: 'He read it through to me in a perturbed sort of way with a gradual crescendo of indignation, in the manner of a man considerably disappointed with what he had written. As soon as he came to the last word he closed up the manuscript violently.' And yet all the time Gilbert had been reading *Trial by Jury*, Sullivan had been splitting his sides with laughter. Sullivan declared he would be delighted to set the piece to music, at which Gilbert suddenly looked pleased.

Sullivan began composing the score the same day and, by working round the clock, managed to complete it in three weeks. D'Oyly Carte had been impressed by Gilbert's hasty production of *Thespis*; now Gilbert had ample time in which to rehearse the principals and the chorus.

When *Trial by Jury* first appeared as a curtain-raiser to *La Périchole* on March 25, 1875, it had a wonderful reception. The *Daily Telegraph*, having raved about the libretto, said: 'Here in fact is the happiest idea caught to perfection by Mr Arthur Sullivan's music and faultlessly executed by the company. The true enjoyment of laughter has not yet been discovered by those who have not yet seen *Trial by Jury*. The *Times* also appreciated it. 'Many were curious to know what kind of an impression a brief extravaganza, the united effort of two Englishmen, would create immediately after one of the productions... of M. Offenbach... To judge by the unceasing and almost boisterous hilarity which formed a sort of running commentary on the part of the audience, *Trial by Jury* suffered nothing whatever from so dangerous a juxtaposition. On the contrary, it may fairly be said to have borne away the palm.'

A cantata in one act, it was a brilliant spoof of Italian opera and contained several melodies that were very easy to remember. The Learned Judge who walks away with pretty Angelina, the Plaintiff, at the end of the breach of promise case, was played by Frederic Sullivan, Arthur's brother, who gave an outstanding performance. His best song relating how he had risen to eminence in the Law after starting out as a briefless barrister, began:

> When I, good friends, was called to the bar,
> I'd an appetite fresh and hearty,
> But I was as many young barristers are,
> An impecunious party.
> I'd a swallow-tail coat of a beautiful blue-
> A brief which I bought of a booby-
> A couple of shirts and a collar or two,
> And a ring that looked like a ruby!

> In Westminster Hall I danced a dance,
> Like a semi-despondent fury;
> For I thought I should never hit on a chance
> Of addressing a British jury –
> But I soon got tired of third class journeys
> And dinners of bread and water,
> So I fell in love with a rich attorney's
> Elderly, ugly daughter.

It was soon obvious that hordes of people were coming to the Royalty on purpose to see *Trial by Jury*, though it was only billed as a curtain-raiser. D'Oyly Carte took *La Périchole* off, and Madame Dolaro followed it with another light opera from her repertoire, but *Trial by Jury* ran on. Carte only withdrew it after 200 performances owing to the tragic death of Frederic Sullivan, who had played the Judge so brilliantly.

Arthur Sullivan was bowled over by the death of his beloved brother, Fred, at the early age of 39. He made himself responsible for

2. A scene showing the Plaintiff and the Learned Judge in *Trial by Jury,* the first
Gilbert and Sullivan success, produced at the Royalty, Soho, in 1875.

Fred's widow and her young children; a few years later he adopted
Fred's eldest son, Herbert Sullivan, and made him his heir. Sullivan
couldn't face any normal work for several weeks afterwards, but he
poured out his affection for Fred in his famous song, 'The Lost Chord'.
After Miss Antoinette Stirling had introduced it to the public, 'The
Lost Chord' became the most popular song of the day.

London society were privileged to hear 'The Lost Chord' sung by
Mrs Fanny Ronalds in her beautiful contralto voice. This highly
attractive lady from Boston, who had only recently come to England,
became Sullivan's closest woman friend. She had been separated from
her American husband, Pierre Ronalds, for several years; according to
a contemporary American newspaper, 'the husband neglected his
wife and disappeared for months at a time. She had to look to her
brave men friends for sympathy and these she found in abundance.'

She had a lovely face with small, very regular features, long dark
brown hair and brown eyes. Fanny Ronalds was wealthy, dressed
superbly, and lived up to her reputation of being a femme fatale.
Amongst the men she had bewitched in New York was Leonard
Jerome, the financier, and father of Lady Randolph Churchill; for a
short time she had been in Paris, where she had been an ornament at
the Court of the Emperor Louis Napoleon.

23

She made her home at 7, Cadogan Place, where she established the most distinguished music salon in London. Leading musicians gladly performed for Mrs Ronalds without a fee, unknown geniuses never refused one of her invitations. Edward, Prince of Wales often came to her musical parties, and the Duke of Edinburgh was another regular visitor to Cadogan Place. Being an intimate friend of the Prince of Wales and Princess Alexandra, Fanny Ronalds was persona grata at Marlborough House, being sometimes known as the unofficial ambassadress at the Court of St James's.

Fanny Ronalds was ten years older than Arthur Sullivan; he looked up to her and consulted her in all matters concerning the social and musical side of his life. Later, she used to accompany him to the theatre when auditions were being held for the comic operas; she would sit in a box and Sullivan generally took her opinion on singers. She acted as hostess whenever he gave a party at Queens' Mansions and people saw them together in her box at Covent Garden and at fashionable race meetings. She and Sullivan were inseparable, if either of them had to go away from London, they would send telegrams and write letters to each other every day. If no letter or telephone call came from her, his day was spoiled.

Arthur Sullivan kept a private diary, in which he used a code of his own. 'L.W.' stood for Little Woman; once it had referred to Rachel Scott Russell, but later on it generally signified Fanny Ronalds. Although his diary was kept under lock and key, and quoted very discreetly by his nephew, Herbert Sullivan, in his biography, there is enough evidence in his diary with its timing of private appointments at Cadogan Place and the curious sex symbols that he used to make it almost certain that Mrs Ronalds was his mistress. Sullivan may have wanted to marry her, but her husband, Pierre Ronalds, never divorced her; in any case if he had married a divorced woman it would have created a terrible scandal and might have ruined his position as England's Composer Laureate. The Victorians were hypocrites who pretended not to notice a case of adultery or any other liaison so long as they were conducted discreetly.

Trial by Jury was revived at the Strand with a new cast, then transferred to the Opéra Comique. D'Oyly Carte, more confident than ever that Gilbert and Sullivan had a great future, formed a syndicate in 1877 with a capital of £6,000 for the production of their comic operas at the Opéra Comique. Each of the syndicate put up £500 and there were four directors: Tom Chappell and George Metzler, both music publishers, Augustus Drake Collard, a piano manufacturer, and Edward Hodgson Bailey, generally known as 'Watercart' Bailey because he had a virtual monopoly of the water-carts used for cleaning the streets of London. Michael Gunn, an Irish music publisher and theatre manager, was one of the original members of the syndicate. At first Carte became secretary and adviser to the Comic Opera syndicate; later, he became managing director.

The Sorcerer, their first production, had been adapted from W.S. Gilbert's story, *The Elixir of Love*. The leading part of John Wellington Wells, 'dealer in magic and spells', had been written specially for the late Frederic Sullivan, so they had to find another actor. Arthur Sullivan spotted George Grossmith playing the Judge in *Trial by Jury* at a charity performance. He spoke to Grossmith, a well known concert entertainer, at his home and said: 'Are you inclined to go on the stage for a time? There is a part in the new piece I am doing with Gilbert which I think you could play admirably. I can't find a good man for it.' At first Grossmith turned down the part. He was rather undersized and had a limited singing voice, and felt incapable of taking a major role on the professional stage.

However, Sullivan arranged for him to meet Gilbert. Grossmith began by saying, 'In the part of the magician, I thought you required a fine man with a large voice.' Gilbert replied humorously, 'No, that's just what we *don't* want!' He liked to mould the artistes to his individual style of ensemble acting, and did his best to make each of the principals give the interpretation of the character that he wanted down to the exact inflection of every word. D'Oyly Carte signed up George Grossmith at a salary of 15 guineas a week, after Grossmith had asked for 3 guineas more, which turned out to be one of the greatest bargains in the history of the English theatre. The directors of the Comic Opera syndicate, whose knowledge of musical plays was limited, sent Carte a wire saying: 'On no account engage Grossmith!'

25

But fortunately it was too late by then.

Another leading actor engaged for the piece was Rutland Barrington, a big man with plenty of confidence, who made an excellent contrast to George Grossmith. Barrington's voice was below operatic standards. He and Grossmith were old comrades, both having at one time been members of Mrs Howard Paul's touring company. Mrs Howard Paul, who was appearing as Lady Sangazure in *The Sorcerer*, had strongly advised Grossmith and Barrington to join the new company.

The Sorcerer revolved around the character of John Wellington Wells, who gives the inhabitants of an English village a love philtre in a teapot, which has the effect of turning all their lives upside down. Everybody wakes up and falls in love with the first person they see (a situation that Gilbert may have borrowed from *A Midsummer Night's Dream*). The villagers have to summon back John Wellington Wells to ask him to restore them to their old selves. The only way he can disenchant everybody is by sacrificing himself to Ahrimanes, a devil.

The Sorcerer opened at the Opera Comique on November 2, 1877; Gilbert had produced it superbly and Sullivan's score made the most of every humorous situation. The piece pleased the critics. The *Times* said, 'Messrs W.S. Gilbert and Arthur Sullivan had once again combined their efforts with the happiest result. A more careful first performance of a new work has rarely been witnessed ... Above all, the music is spontaneous, appearing invariably to spring out of dramatic situations ... it is also distinguished by marked character and skilfully varied in accordance with the nature of the incidents the composer has had to illustrate.'

George Grossmith as John Wellington Wells achieved stardom in a night; the *Punch* critic wrote: 'Mr George Grossmith is the Sorcerest Sorcerer that ever I did see or hear. His incantation song, his clear and intelligible patter song...are things which alone would repay a second visit to the Opera-Comique.'

His patter song began:

Oh, my name is John Wellington Wells,

I'm a dealer in magic and spells,
In blessings and curses,
And ever-filled purses
In prophecies, witches and knells.

If you want a proud foe to 'make tracks' –
If you'd melt a rich uncle in wax –
You've but to look in
At our resident Djinn,
Number seventy, Simmery Axe.

Rutland Barrington received excellent notices for his portrayal of Dr Daly, the slightly amorous vicar, and Mrs Howard Paul as Lady Sangazure also came in for praise. For the first time Gilbert created a woman of uncertain age who makes herself rather ridiculous as a principal character. However, a pompous notice in *Figaro* upset Arthur Sullivan for a long time: 'We must confess to a sense of disappointment at the downward art course Mr Sullivan appears to be drifting into . . . He has all the ability to make him a great composer, but he wilfully throws his opportunities away.'

Despite its merits, *The Sorcerer* was only a moderate success and came off after 177 performances. Had it not been for the tenacity of D'Oyly Carte it would have come off earlier. Every time the box office receipts went down, the hard-headed directors of the syndicate had proposed to put up the notices, and Carte had had to exert all his influence to persuade them to let the piece continue. During its run Gilbert and Sullivan had written another comic opera, *H.M.S. Pinafore*. Based on three of the Bab Ballads, the libretto poked fun at the British Navy, which was then the finest in the world, and had a leading character – Sir Joseph Porter – who was First Lord of the Admiralty although he had never been to sea in his life.

W.S. Gilbert was an all-round man of the theatre; he not only produced the pieces he wrote, but also designed the sets and supervised the costumes. He and Sullivan travelled down to Portsmouth to inspect the naval ships. Then Gilbert went aboard the *Victory* and drew detailed sketches of the quarter deck; he used Nelson's flagship as a model for the set of *H.M.S. Pinafore*. But when he sent Sullivan the first lyrics, the composer was suffering from his kidney complaint, and had been forced to rest. He composed the music for *Pinafore* in between several bad bouts, yet nobody would have guessed from his sparkling score that parts of it had been written while he was in agony.

George Grossmith was a natural choice to play Sir Joseph Porter, the First Lord, while Rutland Barrington had one of his best parts as Captain Corcoran of the *Pinafore*, who hardly ever swore a big, big 'D'. Little Buttercup, the mature bumboat woman who had once been a 'baby farmer', was played by Harriet Everard, a newcomer to Gilbert and Sullivan. Carte hoped that *H.M.S. Pinafore* would be a great success and put the Comic Opera syndicate on a secure financial footing. But the philistine directors of the syndicate only judged a piece by its box office receipts. This factor very nearly wrecked the whole Gilbert and Sullivan enterprise. The other snag was that the Opéra Comique was an out-of-date playhouse which had four entrances to it from different streets off the Strand; anyone who approached from the main entrance in the Strand had to walk through a long, narrow tunnel in order to get to the stalls.

Gilbert once said to a friend, 'Sullivan and I have the same sense of humour. When I tell him a joke he understands it immediately. I never have to tell it twice, which is fatal.' The collaborators were in good spirits when the curtain rose on the quarter-deck of *H.M.S. Pinafore* on May 28, 1878, while D'Oyly Carte, after seeing the dress rehearsal, had no doubt at all that this piece would put their comic operas on the map.

CHAPTER FOUR

PINAFORE MANIA

A hundred thousand barrel organs have been constructed to play nothing but Pinafore.

ARTHUR SULLIVAN

W.S. Gilbert had modelled Sir Joseph Porter, First Lord of the Admiralty, on W.H. Smith, founder of the well known stationers, who had been appointed First Lord in Disraeli's Tory Government although he had never been to sea. The character in the piece was a Radical politician who believed that all men were equal and that all ranks should be abolished; so Gilbert naively imagined that nobody would recognize Sir Joseph as W.H. Smith, who was a true blue Tory. He wrote to Sullivan: 'The fact that the First Lord is a Radical of the most pronounced kind will do away with any suspicion that W.H. Smith is intended.' But a few days after the piece had opened Disraeli nicknamed his First Lord of the Admiralty 'Pinafore' Smith.

The critics hailed *Pinafore* as the best Gilbert and Sullivan opera so far. The *New Era* said: 'As a humorous effort we consider that *H.M.S. Pinafore* surpasses all its predecessors ... Mr Gilbert and Mr Sullivan have worked together in the true spirit of collaboration. The former's ... words are really wedded to the music, not sacrificed to it. Mr Sullivan has entered thoroughly into the spirit of the jest.' And the *Times* wrote: 'Few theatres can boast of such a trio of genuine humorists as Mr George Grossmith (Sir Joseph Porter), Mr Rutland Barrington (Captain Corcoran) and Miss Harriet Everard (Little Buttercup).'

Sir Joseph Porter's song relating how he came to be First Lord thoroughly deserved all the encores:

When I was a lad I served a term
As office boy to an attorney's firm,

I cleaned the windows and I scrubbed the floors,
And I polished up the handle on the big front door.
And I polished up that handle so carefullee
That now I am the ruler of the Queen's Navee!

As office boy I made such a mark
That they gave me the post of a junior clerk.
I served the writs with a smile so bland,
And I copied all the letters in a big round hand –
And I copied all the letters in a hand so free
That now I am the ruler of the Queen's Navee!

Other hits on the first night were 'I am the Captain of the *Pinafore*,' 'He is an Englishman' and 'Never Mind the Why and Wherefore'. The latter was a trio sung by Sir Joseph Porter, Captain Corcoran and his daughter, Josephine, the reluctant fiancée of Sir Joseph.

Though the notices of *Pinafore* had been splendid, D'Oyly Carte began to worry because the box office takings went down every week. One day in July his acting manager, George Edwardes, a handsome young Irishman with charming manners and the gift of the gab, reported that *Pinafore* was only taking £40 a night. London was in the throes of a boiling hot summer, and people fought shy of walking through tunnels to a theatre which was stifling hot inside. But apart from that, the public couldn't appreciate the new, topsy-turvy humour of Gilbert and Sullivan.

The philistine directors of the syndicate kept putting up the notices of *Pinafore*; D'Oyly Carte had to go and see them every week and talk them into agreeing to cancel them. The only director on whom he could rely was Tom Chappell. After a very bad week Carte called a meeting of the company and persuaded them to take a cut of a third of their salaries; even then the directors were still agitating to take *Pinafore* off. Carte had to argue with them for hours, trying to convince them that the piece would be a success in the end if they would only agree to 'nurse' it for a few more weeks. He was expending so much nervous energy in his efforts to keep the comic opera running that it was making him ill.

At the end of the month Arthur Sullivan conducted a Covent

3. Richard D'Oyly Carte, the impresario whose flair brought about the great partnership of Gilbert and Sullivan. He built the Savoy Theatre as a permanent home for their comic operas.

Garden promenade concert and happened to play a selection of music from *H.M.S. Pinafore*; to his delight it was encored five times. Next morning the box office at the Opéra Comique was besieged by people trying to book seats for *Pinafore*. It became the hit of the season and the country began to suffer from *Pinafore* mania: thousands of barrel organs were churning out its tunes, touring companies were perform-

4. Sir William Gilbert wrote fourteen comic operas with Sullivan, ten of which were produced at the Savoy. He thought his plays more important than his musical pieces and resented being knighted twenty years after Sullivan.

ing it all over the British Isles, and hundreds of amateur companies were seeking D'Oyly Carte's permission to produce it. Everybody was whistling Sullivan's tunes and people at last saw the point of Gilbert's jokes.

When *H.M.S. Pinafore* was still playing to capacity, Carte heard from the States that musical 'pirates' had copied the score of *Pinafore*

5. Sir Arthur Sullivan, whose comic operas became a British institution while his serious music was soon forgotten. Queen Victoria made him Master of the Queen's Music.

and it was being performed all over America. The Philadelphia correspondent of the *Times* reported on March 18, 1879: '*H.M.S. Pinafore* has fairly taken our leading cities by storm. In Philadelphia it has been successfully running at half a dozen theatres at one time. In New York and Boston it has been similarly successful . . . and it is running in the South and West . . . Such a furore as this opera has

33

created I have never known before in the history of the American stage.'

News reached Carte that *Pinafore* was being performed in New York by eight different companies, who were using the original music but improvising librettos which were completely inappropriate. It annoyed Carte so much that he resolved to take his own company over to New York to show the Americans an authentic production of *Pinafore*. Meanwhile the members of the syndicate had been raking in the shekels from *Pinafore* from an original investment of £500. D'Oyly Carte had had more than enough of the syndicate; by the end of the summer he was in such a strong position that he bought them out and entered into partnership with Gilbert and Sullivan for the production of all their future operas. The three partners put up £1,000 each and signed an agreement stating that, after deducting necessary expenses, profits were to be divided equally between them. The directors of the syndicate took umbrage at being left out in the cold while *Pinafore* was booming and, under the leadership of 'Water-cart' Bailey, they planned to try and get their revenge.

'The Battle of the Opéra Comique' was fought on July 31 in the middle of a performance of *H.M.S. Pinafore*. The company suddenly heard a great commotion backstage, followed by shouts of 'Come on! Now's the time!' Bailey had sent a gang of thugs to the theatre with orders to seize the scenery. The thugs appeared at the prompt entrance to the stage, terrifying the ladies of the chorus. But the stage hands and the male choristers, led by Richard Barker, the stage manager, joined battle with the 'boarding party'. While sounds of scuffling and loud yells could be heard behind the scenes, Harriet Everard, playing Little Buttercup, bravely went on singing her number. Then Alfred Cellier, the conductor, stopped the performance. George Grossmith, wearing his uniform as Sir Joseph Porter, came forward to the footlights and told the audience to keep calm and remain in their seats.

A free fight was taking place backstage as the thugs tried to steal the scenery of *Pinafore*. But the home team of stage hands and choristers, led by Barker, stood firm and in the end they defeated the raiders and threw them out of the stage door. The only casualty of the battle was Barker, who had been knocked down and seriously injured, but the home team had won the day and saved the scenery, and the company finished their performance to loud cheers from the audience.

After losing 'The Battle of the Opéra Comique', the syndicate presented a rival production of *H.M.S. Pinafore* at the Aquarium Theatre, Westminster. This very inferior effort only ran for 91 performances. Then the syndicate played their last card and had the cheek to transfer their production of *Pinafore* to the Olympic Theatre, next door to the Opéra Comique where it was playing. It failed ignominiously and convinced 'Water-Cart' Bailey and the others that it was time to throw in the sponge.

Arthur Sullivan had been suffering so badly from his kidney complaint that he arranged to have an operation in the autumn. He said at the end of a letter to John Hollingshead, written from Paris:

I have been suffering martyrdom here for a fortnight, but on Monday last I underwent the operation of having the kidney crushed, and I am now well enough to leave Paris to-morrow en route for rest and quiet in the Engadine.

D'Oyly Carte sailed to America with Arthur Sullivan and W.S. Gilbert in *S.S. Bothnia* in November; they had come over to supervise the authentic production of *H.M.S. Pinafore* at the Fifth Avenue Theatre, New York. The genuine *Pinafore* won golden opinions, but unfortunately most New Yorkers had already seen one of the 'pirate' versions and were conspicious by their absence, so the piece only ran for a few weeks. Meanwhile Gilbert and Sullivan had made good progress on a comic opera entitled *The Pirates of Penzance*, partly because Gilbert had been having so much trouble from music pirates in the past year that he was getting his own back.

Carte thought it would be a good piece of showmanship to hold its premiere in New York at the end of the year and duly announced it. The only snag was that Sullivan had left his vital sketches for Act 1 in London, which meant he had a monumental task to write the entire first act before the end of the year. In a letter to his mother on December 8 he said, 'I am writing day and night on the first Act ... the fact is I left all my sketches for the first Act at home ... I would have telegraphed for them, but they would not have arrived in time.'

Thanks to his marvellous memory, Sullivan was able to reproduce the music of Act 1 almost note for note and to deliver it in time for Gilbert to rehearse it with the company; Gilbert had had to put Act 2 into rehearsal first, while waiting for the beginning of Sullivan's score. The only number which had defeated Sullivan was for the first entrance of Major-General Stanley's daughters; he solved the problem by using 'Climbing over rocky mountains', a number he had written for *Thespis*. In order to finish his score, Sullivan had to work all Boxing Day and noted in his diary that he was working till 5.30 in the morning.

He and Alfred Cellier, the conductor, who was also an accomplished composer, had been great friends ever since they had been school fellows at the Chapel Royal. As soon as the dress rehearsal had finished, Sullivan and Cellier wrote the Overture of *The Pirates of Penzance* together. To speed things up, W.S. Gilbert lent a hand and copied out the band parts with Fred Clay, the composer, who happened to be in New York at that time.

Gilbert's targets in *The Pirates of Penzance* were the British Army – which was supposed to have been out of date since Waterloo – and the Police Force. *The Pirates* was produced at the Fifth Avenue without George Grossmith, or Rutland Barrington, or the other leading lights, who had remained in London in *H.M.S. Pinafore*, but the company in America gave excellent performances on the first night, with the sole exception of the tenor who played Frederic. The Broadway critics had nothing but praise for *The Pirates*. The *Sun* reported that 'Its success was instantaneous . . . the performance was constantly stopped by the laughter and applause that attended the humorous parts . . . Mr Sullivan has evidently spared no pains to prevent himself from falling behind his previous reputation, and has given *The Pirates* an even more elaborate and carefully written score, and a broader and more scholarly treatment, than he brought to the composition of *Pinafore*.' Sullivan wrote in his diary: 'House crammed with the elite of New York. Went into the orchestra more dead than alive, but got better when I took the stick in my hand – fine

H. M. S. Pinafore.

6. George Grossmith as the autocratic Sir Joseph Porter being consoled by Cousin Hebe (Jessie Bond) in *H.M.S. Pinafore*, which founded the fortunes of the Gilbert and Sullivan operas.

reception. Grand success.'

One member of the company had nearly ruined the piece: Hugh Talbot, the tenor, who made nonsense of his part of Frederic, the pirate orphan, forgetting his lines and singing off key. In the ordinary way he would have been sacked on the spot, but tenors were a rare commodity in New York, and it took D'Oyly Carte four months to find another tenor. Arthur Sullivan paid this tribute to W.S. Gilbert in a letter to his mother: 'The libretto is ingenious, clever, wonderfully funny in parts, and sometimes brilliant in dialogue – beautifully written for music, as in all Gilbert does.'

As D'Oyly Carte and the two collaborators saw the old year out, they had good reason to expect *The Pirates of Penzance* to repeat its success in London later. Only two years after he had formed the Comic Opera syndicate, Carte had fulfilled his ambition to establish Gilbert and Sullivan operas in England, and in addition he had launched them on an international scale. He and Gilbert and Sullivan had worked together in great harmony in their musical enterprise, and at this moment Carte would not have changed places with anyone in the world.

PART 2
The Savoy Triumvirate

CHAPTER FIVE

MONARCHS OF THE SAVOY

The starting of English opera in a theatre devoted to that alone was the scheme of my life.

RICHARD D'OYLY CARTE

Having launched *The Pirates of Penzance* on Broadway, D'Oyly Carte gave a copyright performance of the piece in England in January. His number one touring company had the distinction of playing *The Pirates* for the first time in England at the Bijou Theatre at Paignton, Devonshire. They had been performing *H.M.S. Pinafore* at Torquay and, after a short rehearsal, were rushed off to Paignton to give *The Pirates of Penzance* at a matinee. Sullivan's score for Act 1, finished at the eleventh hour, had only just arrived from the States. The small matinee audience at the Bijou Theatre witnessed the bizarre spectacle of the actors and actresses playing *The Pirates of Penzance* in their *Pinafore* costumes, wearing coloured handkerchiefs to indicate they were pirates, and singing their music from band parts.

The proceedings had been organized by Helen Lenoir, who had been put in charge of the London office while Carte was in America. She and George Edwardes, the acting manager, got along like a house on fire. Years later, when Edwardes had become the leading impresario of musical plays, he paid many tributes to Helen Lenoir and said she had taught him almost everything he knew about the business side of the theatre. Later in the year, Carte summoned Helen Lenoir to New York to help him organize the American touring companies of *The Pirates of Penzance*; then he appointed her his American representative and she stayed over there for the next six years.

W.S. Gilbert began rehearsing the regular company in *The Pirates of Penzance* as soon as *Pinafore* came off at the Opéra Comique after a record run of 700 performances. Gilbert had written most of the parts specially for the artistes who had more or less

41

formed themselves into the D'Oyly Carte repertory company. The role of Major-General Stanley, an Army counterpart of Sir Joseph Porter, was tailor-made for George Grossmith; Rutland Barrington acted the small but most effective part of the Sergeant of Police; Richard Temple, who had been Dick Deadeye in *Pinafore*, made a splendid Pirate King; and George Power, who had been Ralph *Rackstraw in Pinafore,* played Frederic, the pirate orphan. While Harriet Everard, who had been Little Buttercup, was an obvious choice for Ruth, the pirate maid-of-all-work who has reached mature years.

People had begun to notice Gilbert's bias in the comic operas against women who were no longer in their first youth. He once sat next to a lady of uncertain age at a dinner party and said to her, 'You remember the Crimean War, don't you?' 'Certainly not!' she said indignantly. 'Oh, I'm sure you could if you tried!' Gilbert retorted.

At one of the last rehearsals of *The Pirates of Penzance* Harriet Everard, as Ruth, was standing in the middle of the stage when a set piece fell forward and fractured her skull. Emily Cross had to take over the part from her at twenty four hours' notice and acquitted herself very well on the first night. But poor Miss Everard never recovered from her injury and died later.

The Pirates of Penzance opened at the Opéra Comique on April 3, 1880, and was an instant success. The public had caught on to the humour of Gilbert and Sullivan at last. The *Standard* remarked: 'How completely Mr Sullivan enters into the spirit of his companion's words has been acknowledged again and again; and here even the simplest airs are rescued from being commonplace by the piquant and skilful orchestration.' And the *Times* gave Barrington a special mention: 'Mr Rutland Barrington was absolutely sublime in the small but important part of the Sergeant of Police.'

Rutland Barrington had sensibly agreed to play the Sergeant of Police although he only appeared for 17 minutes in the second Act. George Grossmith triumphed as Major-General Stanley; lovely Marion Hood as his daughter Mabel charmed the house with her rendering of 'Poor wandering one', and Rutland Barrington stopped the show when he sang 'A policeman's lot is not a happy one':

When a felon's not engaged in his employment,
Or maturing his felonious little plans,
His capacity for innocent enjoyment
Is just as great as any other man's.
Our feelings we with difficulty smother
When constabulary duty's to be done.
Ah! take one consideration with another
A policeman's lot is not a happy one!

George Grossmith also got encored for his song about an out of date modern major-general:

I am the very pattern of a modern major-gineral,
I've information vegetable, animal and mineral;
I know the kings of England, and I quote the fights historical,
From Marathon to Waterloo, in order categorical;
I'm very well acquainted, too, with matters mathematical;
I understand equations, both the single and quadrilateral;
About binomial theorem I'm teeming with a lot of news;
With many cheerful facts about the square of the hypoteneuse.
I'm very good at integral and differential calculus,
I know the scientific names of beings animalculous;
In short, in matters vegetable, animal and mineral
I am the very model of a modern major-gineral.

The Pirates had such a long run that Gilbert and Sullivan had plenty of time to start writing a new comic opera. Gilbert based his libretto on 'The Rival Curates', one of his Bab Ballads, but then decided that the public might think him irreverent if he made a laughing stock of curates, particularly as he had been adversly criticised for his portrait of Dr Daly, the vicar in *The Sorcerer*. He therefore changed the characters into two rival poets, typical of the freakish elements in the Aesthetic Movement. George du Maurier had already satirised these people in *Punch* and F.C. Burnand had lampooned them in his comedy, *The Colonel*; but that didn't stop

Gilbert tackling the same subject. Although "The Colonel" appeared before "Patience", W. S. Gilbert put a note in the programme that "Patience" had been written before "The Colonel" was produced. Bunthorne and Grosvenor, the rival poets in *Patience*, were caricatures of well known aesthetes of the day, Bunthorne being a mixture of Oscar Wilde and James McNeill Whistler with a dash of Walter Pater, while Grosvenor had been inspired by Charles Algernon Swinburne. George Grossmith was specially made up to look like Wilde and Whistler, and Rutland Barrington was made up like Swinburne.

Unfortunately Arthur Sullivan had promised to deliver his religious work, *The Mayor of Antioch,* for the Leeds Festival in April 1881. This partly explains why he got so late with his score for *Patience*; he worked till 5:00 in the morning for days on end in order to catch up on the comic opera. The first night had been scheduled for April 23, but Sullivan only began scoring with ten days in hand.

The first night audience on April 23 read in their programmes this apologia for satirising the Aesthetic Movement:

> The new movement has latterly given play to the outpourings of a clique of professors of ultra-refinement who preach the gospel of morbid languor and sickly sensuousness which is half real, and half affected by the high priests for the purpose of gaining social notoriety. The authors of *Patience* have not desired to cast ridicule on the true aesthetic spirit, but only to attack the unmanly oddities which masquerade in its likeness.

D'Oyly Carte, with his flair for publicity, had invited Oscar Wilde and James Whistler to the first night of *Patience*. There were screams, yells and hisses as Oscar Wilde, wearing a daffodil in his buttonhole, took his seat in the stalls. The fashionable audience divided their attention between the stage of the Opéra Comique and the stalls, where Wilde and Whistler were sitting together, very curious to observe how the two aesthetes were reacting to Gilbert and Sullivan's satire. The piece went without a hitch and there were eight encores, including 'If you're anxious for to shine', 'Prithee, pretty maiden', 'The magnet and the churn', 'When I first put my uniform on', 'If you want a receipt for that popular mystery' and 'Silvered is the raven hair'.

The press were equally enthusiastic about *Patience*, or *Bunthorne's Bride*: 'The composer's settings of the lyrical portions of Mr Gilbert's witty satire are in nearly every case, bright and melodious', said the *Daily News*. 'The sentiment and grace of most of Mr Sullivan's music gives the additional zest to the quaintness and humour of the other portions, and there is little doubt that these qualities and merits of Mr Gilbert's book will secure a success as great as any that hitherto resulted from the same co-operation.'

The most devastating number in the piece was sung by George Grossmith as the poet Bunthorne:

If you're anxious for to shine in a high aesthetic line as a
man of culture rare,
You must get up all the germs of the transcendental terms,
and plant them everywhere,
You must lie upon the daisies and discourse in novel phrases
of your complicated state of mind,
The meaning doesn't matter, if it's only idle chatter of a
transcendental kind.

And everyone will say
As you walk your mystic way,
'If this young man expresses himself in terms too deep for
me,
Why, what a very singularly deep young man this deep
young man must be!'

Rutland Barrington as Grosvenor, the rival poet, sang the charming ballad of 'The magnet and the churn':

A magnet hung in a hardware shop,
And all around was a golden crop
Of scissors and needles, nails and knives,
Offering love for all their lives;
But for iron the magnet had no whim,
Though he charmed it, it charmed not him.
From scissors and needles and knives he'd turn
For he'd set his love on a Silver Churn.

Bunthorne   Patience   a Grosven...
Walt... Passmore   Henry Lytton

His most aesthetic,
Very magnetic,
Fancy took this form –
'If I can wheedle
A knife or a needle,
Why not a Silver Churn?'

At the beginning of the year D'Oyly Carte had commissioned C.J. Phipps, the leading theatre architect, to design a new theatre for him in the Strand to house the Gilbert and Sullivan operas. Since it stood on the site of the medieval palace of the Princes of Savoy, he decided to call it the Savoy Theatre. It had seating accommodation for 1,290 people, a great advance on the capacity of the Opéra Comique. Carte, who was still running his concert and lecture agency, had booked Oscar Wilde to go on a lecture tour of the States. Since the American production of *Patience* was to take place while Wilde was over there, he spoke to him and hinted that it would be appreciated if the poet gave the piece a little bit of publicity. He wrote to Helen Lenoir in New York that 'Wilde is slightly sensitive, but not appallingly so . . . I told him he must not mind my using a little bunkum to push business in America.' Oscar Wilde was most co-operative, and went to several first nights of *Patience* in various cities of America, dressed in his well known aesthetic costume.

The Savoy, Carte's elegant new theatre in the Strand, was completed in October; it was one of the first playhouses to be constructed on the cantilever principle, which enabled audiences to obtain an excellent view of the stage from any seat in the house, and it also had entrances and exits on all sides. Carte made no charge for programmes and initiated the system of having people queue for seats instead of stampeding the box office. *Patience* was transferred to the Savoy on October 10; the Prince of Wales entered the Royal Box to the applause of a crowded house. Afterwards Sullivan took the Prince behind the scenes and introduced him to all the artistes in the Green

◁ 7. Walter Passmore as Bunthorne and Henry Lytton as Grosvenor, the rival aesthetic poets, in a revival of *Patience*. First produced at the Opéra Comique, it was transferred to the Savoy in October 1881.

47

Room. He particularly admired Jessie Bond, who had been in the company since *H.M.S. Pinafore* and was to become the most popular soubrette in the history of Gilbert and Sullivan operas.

D'Oyly Carte was the first manager to install electricity in the auditorium to replace gas lighting. He gambled on the electricity giving them no trouble, but had gas installed in reserve in case of a breakdown. At a matinée on December 28 he illuminated the Savoy stage with electricity for the first time. He came on the stage at the end holding an electric light bulb and gave the audience a short lecture on the safety of electric lighting. Then he placed some muslin over the bulb, like a conjuror, and smashed it to smithereens with a hammer. Carte demonstrated that the muslin was unburnt and was greeted with a round of applause, although one man had fled from the auditorium in fear of his life.

Patience ran on well into 1882; the first mention of their new comic opera appeared in Sullivan's diary: 'Gilbert came this evening and sketched out an idea for a new piece – Lord Chancellor, Peers, Fairies, etc. Funny, but at present vague.' The fairy story developed into an amusing conflict between Arcadian fairies and British peers, and provided Gilbert with a fine excuse to make fun of British politics. His brilliant libretto stimulated Sullivan to write one of his most imaginative scores. In view of the fact that the previous comic operas had been pounced upon by music 'pirates', who made copies of the score before the English premieres, Carte arranged to keep the title of the new piece – *Iolanthe* – a secret till the last moment. The piece was therefore known to the company as *Perola* right up to the day of the dress rehearsal, when Sullivan revealed that the real title was going to be *Iolanthe*. A young actor panicked in case he should sing 'Perola' by mistake and infuriate Mr Gilbert. 'You don't have to worry about Mr Gilbert', the composer assured him. 'He's *never* at his first nights!' This was perfectly true; first nights made Gilbert so nervous that he generally walked up and down the Embankment until it was time to go back to the Savoy to take his curtain call.

Fairies get involved with mortals in the most extraordinary fashion in *Iolanthe*, one example being the mature Fairy Queen, who falls in love with the Sentry at Palace Yard, Westminster. During the second act she calls on Captain Shaw to cool her ardour for the Sentry; it was a topical joke because Captain Massey Shaw was actually the head of the newly formed London Fire Brigade. D'Oyly Carte, with typical showmanship, arranged for Captain Massey Shaw to be sitting in the middle of the stalls at the Savoy on the first night of *Iolanthe* on November 25, 1882. It was therefore an easy matter for the Fairy Queen, played by Alice Barnettn to address these lines to him:

Oh, Captain Shaw,
Type of true love kept under,
Could thy brigade
With cold cascade
Quench my great love, I wonder!

Before Arthur Sullivan left home to conduct the orchestra in *Iolanthe* he heard that he had lost his entire savings of £7,000 because his stockbrokers, Cooper Hall and Co. had gone bankrupt. He had received the following letter:

131 Piccadilly.
25th November.

My dear Arthur,

Perhaps you have learnt by this time that I am hopelessly messed, and that you must for the present look upon your money as lost. God knows how it will end but I have seen it coming for ages.

...I am afraid Cooper is not the man we have always thought him. I have been weak and he has exerted a fatal influence and power over me...Come and see me, my dear boy, though I fear you will hate me.

Yours sincerely,

Edward Hall.

P.S. I nearly went out of my mind on Sunday but am better.

It was a shattering blow for Sullivan, but he managed to control his feelings and drove off to the Savoy and conducted *Iolanthe* as if nothing had happened. When the curtain rose on the fairies blissfully dancing in Arcady, the audience were thrilled to see that the fairies were lit up by electric light bulbs, connected somewhere near the small of their backs. *Iolanthe* was received with rapture and seemed a certain success. However, Sullivan felt very low by the end of the evening.

The influential critic of *Theatre* wrote: 'I do not hesitate to say that the music of *Iolanthe* is Dr Sullivan's chef d'oeuvre . . . In fitting notes to words so exactly that the 'book' and the setting appear to be one and indivisible, our gifted composer is without a rival in England.' George Grossmith was in magnificent form as the highly susceptible Lord Chancellor, who keeps breaking into a dance at the slightest provocation. The *Era* reported that 'Mr George Grossmith as the Lord Chancellor brings all his comic talent and skill to bear upon one of the drollest impersonations imaginable.' Jessie Bond, who had a lovely singing voice, played Iolanthe, the fairy mother who remained seventeen for ever. One critic wrote: 'She may be credited with all the graces, delicacy and fascination we should expect from a fairy mother, and her singing of the really exquisite melody in the last act is one of the most successful items.'

Amongst the most popular numbers in the piece were 'When I went to the Bar as a very young man', 'The March of the Peers', 'The Law is the true embodiment', 'The Sentry's Song' and 'When you're lying awake with a dismal headache', which was sung by George Grossmith as the Lord Chancellor. The latter had one of the most ingenious lyrics ever written by Gilbert, or any other writer:

When you're lying awake with a dismal headache, and repose is taboo'd by anxiety,
I conceive you may use any language you choose to indulge in without impropriety;
For your brain is on fire – the bed clothes conspire of usual slumbers to plunder you;
First your counterpane goes and uncovers your toes, and your

sheet slips demurely from under you;
Then the blanketing tickles – you feel like mixed pickles – so
terrribly sharp is the pricking.
And you're hot and you're cross, and you tumble and toss till
there's nothing 'twixt you and the ticking.
Then the bedclothes all creep to the ground in a heap, and
you pick 'em all up in a tangle;
Next your pillow resigns and politely declines to remain at
its usual angle!

Iolanthe had a long stay at the Savoy and brought substantial
profits to the triumvirate, with the result that Arthur Sullivan began
to recover his Stock Exchange losses far sooner than he had dared to
hope. The 'eighties were destined to be the most successful decade of
all for the Gilbert and Sullivan operas.

CHAPTER SIX

MAKE WAY FOR THE MIKADO

Nothing fresher, gayer or more captivating has ever bid for public favour than this delightful composition.

THEATRE REVIEW OF *THE MIKADO*, MARCH 1885.

Arthur Sullivan celebrated his fortieth birthday on May 13 during the run of *Iolanthe* and held a big party for the event at Queens' Mansions. Mrs Fanny Ronalds acted as hostess and Edward, Prince of Wales, was among the guests. Sullivan produced a novel surprise for the occasion: he had arranged for a new machine called an electrophone to be placed on the stage of the Savoy during the performance of *Iolanthe* to record the sound of the comic opera. He made a telephone call to the theatre as the curtain went up and kept the line open to the Savoy throughout the performance; so his guests heard the piece all through from the overture to the finale.

Sullivan often invited George Grossmith, Rutland Barrington, Jessie Bond and other Savoy artistes to his parties, and sometimes they entertained the guests by singing for them. Edward, Prince of Wales, whose interest in the fair sex has become legendary, lost no time in asking Jessie Bond if he could come and visit her one day. 'What for, sir?' she asked. 'My mother would be very surprised if she saw you walking into our house!' Jessie Bond's quick wits had rescued her from the embarrassing attentions of the Prince. He never found out that actually she lived alone in a flat in London and that her mother and father lived miles away from town in the Midlands.

During the year Arthur Sullivan had an acute attack of musical conscience because he had been so busy composing Savoy operas for the past three years that he had not written any serious music. Gilbert decided to base their next piece on *The Princess,* an old burlesque of his which had been a gentle send-up of Tennyson's famous poem. Gilbert had great scorn for the 'new women' who were just starting to take up careers, or opting for higher education at the recently founded colleges of Girton and Newnham. *Princess Ida* was a conventional satire on women's emancipation, adapted in blank verse from his 1870 comedy. The libretto seems inferior to his best work, and one can sympathise with Sullivan for finding it hard to set to music.

On May 22, 1883, Sullivan was knighted for his services to music; it was a well deserved honour as he had done his best to further the cause of British music for nearly twenty years. However, W.S. Gilbert fumed about it. He was undoubtedly the moving spirit in their collaboration and felt he had been passed over because the powers that be had a prejudice against him because he had dared to laugh at British institutions. When the *Musical Review* announced Sullivan's knighthood, they felt bound to remind him of his duty: 'Some things Mr Arthur Sullivan may do, Sir Arthur Sullivan ought not to do. Here is not only an opportunity, but a positive obligation for him to return to the sphere from which he has too long descended.' And his close friend, Sir George Grove, wrote in his Dictionary of Music and Musicians: 'Surely the time has come when so able and experienced a master of music, orchestra and stage effect . . . may rally his gifts to a serious opera on some subject of abiding human or natural interest?'

Sullivan, perhaps because he felt that the composition of *Princess Ida* might prove tedious, kept postponing his start on the piece to the annoyance of Gilbert. Seeking a warmer climate, he departed to the South of France for a short holiday. On his return he heard that the composer Fred Clay, his best friend, had had a paralytic stroke while walking in the Strand with George R. Sims. Next day Clay had a second stroke which left him speechless and in a coma. It upset Sullivan so much that he couldn't work for some weeks. Eventually he started work on the piece, but he was so late that he had to make a tremendous effort to finish his score in time; he was squandering his physical powers.

Gilbert suffered from gout; his complaint had become very painful and made him more bad-tempered than ever at his rehearsals. All the company were on tenderhooks as he drilled them through their parts in order to teach them to play *Princess Ida* in exactly the right way. George Grossmith, an extremely sensitive man, suffered more than any of the principals at these rehearsals; he felt ill at ease in the rather minor role of King Gama and couldn't get used to speaking his lines in blank verse. Gilbert's caustic comments upset him so much that he resorted to drugs and gave himself hypodermic injections in the arm.

Sir Arthur Sullivan generally brought Mrs Ronalds to the final rehearsals at the Savoy; he had a great respect for her judgement on the singing. W.S. Gilbert brought his wife, Lucy, whose opinion he valued on the costumes of the pieces. One day she disappeared from the auditorium and he sent an assistant to find her. The young man returned, looking embarrassed, and said, 'She's round behind, Sir.' 'I know she's round behind!' yelled Gilbert, 'but where *is* she?'

It was unfortuntae that neither Gilbert or Sullivan felt at home in the other's company. They were both rather nervous in the effort to be pleasant to each other with the result that they behaved with a bonhomie that never quite rang true. Gilbert once said to Maud Tree: 'Sullivan never says much to me, and what he *does* say, I usually knock a lot off of, for discount.'

Sometimes rehearsals with Gilbert became so acrimonious that a deep depression settled over the company. They tried to clear the air by calling in George Edwardes, the acting manager, an expert at pouring oil on troubled waters. 'Send for Edwardes' became quite a catchword at the Savoy. The staff treated Gilbert with great respect, but Edwardes, though he admired him tremendously as a producer, refused to kow-tow to him. Gilbert resented the way Edwardes stood up to him and even tried to get him sacked. But D'Oyly Carte, who thought a great deal of George Edwardes, ignored Gilbert's complaints and kept him on at the theatre.

In order to complete the score of *Princess Ida* in time, Sullivan had had to work at impossible hours. By the end of the year he was all in. With *Princess Ida* due to open in a few days, his doctor ordered him to bed. Nobody expected Sullivan to be able to conduct the piece on the first night on January 5, 1884, so Carte had a slip put in the programme to say that Francois Cellier would conduct *Princess Ida*. But in the afternoon Sullivan forced himself to get out of bed, drugged himself with morphia, and gave himself a cup of black coffee to keep him awake. To everyone's astonishment he arrived at the Savoy just in time to conduct the Overture. 'After the performance I turned very faint and could hardly stand', Sullivan said in his diary; it was hardly surprising.

The story of *Princess Ida* is not very well known. She has been married to Prince Hilarion in infancy, but when the royal couple grow up Princess Ida forswears men and founds a university for women at Castle Adamant. When her father, King Gama, tells King Hildebrand, Hilarion's father, that their union cannot take place, the latter falls into a rage, imprisons Gama and his sons, and sends Prince Hilarion to Castle Adamant to fetch back Princess Ida. The Prince and his friends get into the castle disguised as women, but they are soon unmasked. King Hildebrand threatens to destroy Castle Adamant next day unless Ida marries Hilarion and King Gama also pleads with Princess Ida to give in and get married. Ida's brothers are defeated in battle, Hildebrand raises a logical question, and she agrees to marry Hilarion.

Gilbert had made a mistake in writing weak parts for George Grossmith (King Gama) and Rutland Barrington (King Hilderbrand). The press were not encouraging about *Princess Ida*. *Figaro* thought that the third act 'drags and is from every point the weakest'. Several critics felt the piece was too long, one found it downright dull, and Edmund Yates declared it was 'three and a half hours' misery'. However, the *Theatre* praised Sullivan's music and the *Sunday Times* considered *Princess Ida* his best score.

The public gave its verdict by March, for by then *Princess Ida* was starting to wilt at the Savoy. D'Oyly Carte, therefore, wrote his usual letter to Gilbert and Sullivan, requesting them to start work on a new piece to replace *Princess Ida* in the summer. Sullivan had gone off to the Continent to try and recuperate after the strain of completing the score; his reply to Carte, written from Brussels, came as a bombshell: 'I ought to tell you at once that it is impossible for me to do another piece of the character of those already written by Gilbert and myself. The reason for this I can give you verbally when we meet...'

Carte wrote to Sullivan reminding him that, according to their contract, he and Gilbert were obliged to provide a new piece for the Savoy on request. Should they fail to do so, the collaborators were liable to make up the losses incurred by the management. Gilbert, alarmed by Sullivan's attitude, wrote to him confirming what Carte had said about their liability for losses if they failed to write a new piece.

Sullivan then wrote a letter to Gilbert from Paris on April 2 to clarify the stand he was taking about their comic operas. 'I will be quite frank. With *Princess Ida* I have come to the end of my tether – the end of my capability in that class of piece. My tunes are in danger of becoming mere repetitions of my former pieces . . . It has hitherto been mere word-setting . . . the music is never allowed to rise and speak for itself . . . I should like to set a story of human interest and probability.' He ended more cheerfully – 'I hope with all my heart that there may be no break in our chain of joint workmanship.'

Arthur Sullivan had been forced to realize that he couldn't possibly maintain his present high standard of living by only writing serious music. Whereas he was earning £10,000 a year from the Savoy operas, his last composition for the Leeds Festival had only brought him a fee of 300 guineas, a sum he sometimes lost in a single night's gambling at Monte Carlo. He therefore invited Gilbert to come to his flat to discuss their next comic opera. But Gilbert again proposed his 'lozenge' plot, which Sullivan had rejected two years before because it was too much like the plot of *The Sorcerer*. Sullivan refused point blank to accept the 'lozenge' plot, and Gilbert left him after nothing had been decided.

W.S. Gilbert returned to his sumptuous new house in Harrington Gardens, Kensington, to try and think up a new story. After *Princess Ida* came off at the Savoy, Carte presented revivals of Gilbert and Sullivan operas as a stop-gap. One day when Gilbert was sitting in his library at Harrington Gardens, an antique Japanese sword fell down from the wall with a great crash. It immediately suggested a Japanese story to him, so he sat down at his writing desk, picked up his quill pen and began writing in his plot-book. He had hit on the germ of *The Mikado;* one can argue that this comic opera might never have been written if Sullivan had not stood out and refused to work on the 'lozenge' plot. On hearing the Japanese story, Sullivan accepted it with relief and Gilbert began to write the libretto. Sullivan was enchanted with Gilbert's first lyrics, which he received a few weeks later, and settled down to write the score of *The Mikado* in much better spirits than he had been for a long time.

W.S. Gilbert paid a visit to the Japanese village that had recently been installed in Knightsbridge and engaged a Geisha girl to coach the Savoy company. She taught them all correct Japanese deportment, and showed the ladies how to spread their fans or snap them in anger, and how to giggle and how to hiss. The Geisha girl only knew two words in English – 'Sixpence, please' – which was the price of a cup of coffee at the Japanese Exhibition. Gilbert also engaged Arthur Dóisy of the Japanese legation to supervise the costumes and sets of the new piece.

Rehearsals of *The Mikado* were long and arduous. In the ordinary way Gilbert demanded very high standards from the company, but in this comic opera he also aimed to perfect the Japanese atmosphere. Actresses were sometimes almost in tears before he was satisfied they were interpreting their roles correctly. Durward Lely, who played Nanki-Poo, had a magnificent tenor voice, but his acting was not quite on a par with his singing. At the end of his first scene Gilbert addressed him:

> Very good, Lely, very good indeed, but I have come down from the back seat in the gallery, and there are one or two words which failed to reach me quite distinctly. Sullivan's music is, of course, very beautiful and I heard every note without difficulty, but I think my words are not altogether without merit, and ought to be heard without undue effort...

George Grossmith, who played Ko-Ko, the upstart Lord High Executioner, suffered more than the others under the lash of Gilbert's tongue. At the dress rehearsal Gilbert suddenly announced he was going to cut the Mikado's song, 'My object all sublime'. However, after a deputation of choristers had called on him and begged him to retain the number, he agreed to keep it in. Richard Temple, who gave a memorable performance as the Mikado, scored one of the biggest hits in the piece with 'My object all sublime'.

When Sir Arthur Sullivan began conducting the Overture at the Savoy on March 14, 1885, he knew that all the company were terribly nervous. But the piece went off wonderfully well, apart from a bad start by George Grossmith as Ko-Ko; there were so many encores that the artistes thought the performance would never finish. When George Grossmith made his first entrance as Ko-Ko, he had lost his confidence after so many gruelling rehearsals, and had also nearly lost his voice. He was nothing like his old self in the first Act, but in Act two he kicked up his legs in the air as he started to dance and the audience yelled their applause. Once he had regained his confidence, 'Gee-Gee' gave a flawless performance.

One of Gilbert's friends at the first night remarked that Rutland Barrington as Pooh-Bah, Lord High Everything Else, had sung in tune all the time, a very rare occurrence. 'That was only first night nervousness', Gilbert explained.

The Mikado is generally regarded as the cleverest comic opera in the English language, so one should mention that it was written and produced in nine months. The notices were superlative; the *Theatre* said:

... nothing fresher, gayer or more captivating has ever bid for public favour than this delightful composition... The text of *The Mikado* sparkles with gems of wit, and its author's rhyming and rhythmic gifts have never been more splendidly displayed... *The Mikado* contains half-a-dozen numbers, each of which is sufficiently attractive to ensure the opera's popularity; musical gems of great price...

Rutland Barrington was showered with praise for his portrayal of Pooh-Bah, one of the greatest snobs in light opera; Rosina Brandram received fine notices for her portrayal of the monstrous Katisha, the Mikado's daughter-in-law elect; and Jessie Bond made the most of her role of Pitti-Singh. Jessie Bond, a very small person, asked the wardrobe mistress to give her an obi about twice as big as Leonora Braham wore as Yum-Yum. 'I made the most of my big, big bow', said Jessie Bond, 'turning my back to the audience whenever I got a chance and waggling it. The gallery was delighted, but I nearly got the sack for that prank.'

Amongst the gems in the score were 'A wandering minstrel', 'Three little maids', 'The sun whose rays', 'Tit willow', 'My object all sublime', 'The Flowers that bloom in the spring' and 'I've got a little list'. Durward Lely, as Nanki-Poo, sang 'A Wandering Minstrel' in the first act:

A wandering minstrel I –
A thing of shreds and patches,
Of ballad songs and snatches,
And dreamy lullaby!
My catalogue is long
Through every passion ranging,
And to your fancies changing
I tune my supple song!

Are you in sentimental mood?
I'll sigh with you
Oh, sorrow, sorrow!
On maiden's coldness do you brood?
I'll do so, too –
Oh, sorrow, sorrow!

I'll charm your willing ears
With songs of lovers' fears
While sympathetic tears
My cheeks bedew –
Oh, sorrow, sorrow!

George Grossmith as the Lord High Executioner made a big hit with his number, 'I've got a little list':

As it seems essential that a victim should be found,
I've got a little list – I've got a little list
Of society offenders who might well be underground,
And who never would be missed – who never would be
missed!
There's the pestilential nuisances who write for autographs –
All people who have flabby hands and irritating laughs –
All children who are up in dates and floor you with 'em
flat –

8. Rutland Barrington as Pooh-Bah, his most famous part, in the 1905 revival of *The Mikado* at the Savoy. He had created the role in 1885.

All persons who in shaking hands shake hands with you like
that –
And all third persons who on spoiling tête-à-têtes insist –
They'd none of 'em be missed – they'd none of 'em be
missed!

The Mikado, the most successful of all the Gilbert and Sullivan
operas, was probably also the greatest. It triumphed all over the
English speaking world. D'Oyly Carte wanted to present it in New
York as soon as possible; two Broadway managers made him offers,
but he turned down Duff of the Standard Theatre and agreed to let
Stetson produce it at the Fifth Avenue Theatre, where *H.M.S.
Pinafore* and *The Pirates of Penzance* had been performed. Duff took
umbrage and announced he would put on a 'pirate' version of *The
Mikado* before Carte could produce the original at the Fifth Avenue.

D'Oyly Carte went into action and cabled his New York agent
that he was going to bring over a company and produce the genuine
Mikado on Broadway first. Operating in the manner of a Secret
Service agent, he swore his touring company to silence and booked
their passages from Liverpool to the States in false names, while he
sailed over to New York under the name of 'Mr Harry Chapman'.
They arrived in New York before Duff had any inkling that they were
on the way. After rehearsing for only two days the company presented
The Mikado at the Fifth Avenue on August 19, 1885, and they
received the same wonderful welcome as in London. Carte and Helen
Lenoir sent out touring companies all over the States, while Alfred
Cellier, Carte's musical director in America, supervised a tour of *The
Mikado* in Australia.

A *Mikado* craze started up in America; it seemed as if every other
household had a sanctum known as the *Mikado* room, full of Japanese
knick-knacks. D'Oyly Carte had applied for an injunction to stop
Duff's 'pirate' production of *The Mikado* at the Standard. But when
the case came up Justice Divver ruled against Carte in the following
jingoistic judgement: 'Copyright or no copyright, commercial honesty
or commercial buccaneering, no Englishman possesses any right
which a true born American is bound to respect.'

C. GOODALL & SON LONDON

JACK.

"And in my court I sit all day,
Giving agreeable girls away."—Iolanthe.

Yours faithfully
Geo: Grossmith

As George Edwardes checked the weekly receipts of *The Mikado* at the Savoy, then estimated its profits from America and elsewhere, he could tell that the triumvirate were making a second fortune. He felt he must take stock of his position: he knew that however long he stayed on with D'Oyly Carte he would always be an underling at the theatre. At twenty-nine he yearned for the chance to prove himself as a producer of musical plays. He realized what a wonderful training ground the Savoy had been for him; Carte and Helen Lenoir had taught him the A–Z of the theatre business, and watching Gilbert directing the company had been a great education in stage management.

He had been on friendly terms with John Hollingshead of the Gaiety ever since he had joined Carte at the Opéra Comique, and they had kept in touch since the company moved to the Savoy. Hollingshead liked to hear the latest news about Gilbert and Sullivan, though he regretted letting them go over to D'Oyly Carte. 'Honest John' was nearly sixty and in failing health from rheumatism. The responsibility of running the Gaiety, in addition to his other theatrical interests and his business ventures, had become too much for him. In the spring of 1885 he invited George Edwardes to buy a half share in the theatre and go into partnership with him.

Edwardes went to Hatton Garden and called on his old friend, Mr Isaacs, a diamond merchant at whose house he had stayed when he first came to London from Grimsby. Isaacs thought the world of George Edwardes; having heard about the Gaiety proposition, he wrote him a cheque for the amount he needed. George Edwardes left the Savoy in the summer, much to the regret of D'Oyly Carte and Sir Arthur Sullivan, although Gilbert was probably glad to see the back of him. Edwardes had arranged to marry Julia Gwynne, one of the most attractive soubrettes in the Savoy company. Edwardes received this letter from Sullivan soon after he had left:

◁ 9. A cartoon by Jack of George Grossmith in the role of the susceptible Lord Chancellor in *Iolanthe,* produced at the Savoy in 1882.

1, Queens Mansions,
   Victoria Street,
      S.W.   23rd September, 1885.

Dear Mr. Edwardes,

I was much gratified by your kind note...Your
departure from the Savoy Theatre is a matter of very
great regret to myself and I am sure to my colleagues
also, since we lose in you a faithful and loyal adherent.

And I need hardly say that you carry with you into
your new undertaking our heartiest good wishes for your
success and welfare. I am sending you a little souvenir
which I hope you will accept in remembrance of our
connection.

                           Yours sincerely,
                           Arthur Sullivan.

Sullivan enclosed a charming collection of illustrations of the Savoy
operas from *Patience* to *The Mikado* which George Edwardes
treasured all his life. Edwardes had married Julia Gwynne on July 9th
at the Catholic church of Corpus Christi in Maiden Lane. After they
had spent their honeymoon at Bournemouth, Julia Gwynne left to go
off on a provincial tour in straight plays with Mr and Mrs Bancroft's
company, and Edwardes joined John Hollingshead at the Gaiety. He
always kept in close touch with D'Oyly Carte and Helen Lenoir
afterwards, sometimes asking their advice about productions. Within
a few years of his arrival at the Gaiety, George Edwardes was to
revolutionize the style of London's musical plays.

CHAPTER SEVEN

GAIETY GEORGE

(George Edwardes) cast himself in every new play, in the part of the public, and he watched the production with one foot in the pit, and the other in the front row of the stalls.

PAUL RUBENS, THE *STAGE*, OCTOBER 1915

George Edwardes, who had developed a flair for knowing what the public wanted, had no doubt they were tired of the burlesques that John Hollingshead had been presenting at the Gaiety for the last seventeen years; the comedians in them hurled outrageous puns at the audience and spoke in doggerel verse, and the curvaceous chorus girls stood at the stage, ogling the mashers, in tatty tights from the theatre wardrobe. Edwardes knew that this entertainment could never stand up to the competition of light operas by Gilbert and Sullivan or Offenbach or other leading composers. Times had changed since the great days when the Gaiety Quartette, consisting of Nellie Farren, Edward Terry, Katie Vaughan and Edward Royce, had delighted audiences and brought 'House Full' notices to the theatre. Katie Vaughan, Edward Terry and Edward Royce had deserted Hollingshead for other engagements, leaving Nellie Farren as his only star. This marvellous little artiste, though well over forty, remained the best male impersonator in the business, and still cavorted about the stage like a young girl. She was the uncrowned queen of the Gaiety and the boys in the gallery simply adored her.

At the time George Edwardes became his partner, Hollingshead was preparing to produce *Little Jack Shepherd,* a burlesque of the notorious highwayman which made a perfect vehicle for Nellie Farren. The only problem was to find a first class comedian to play opposite her. Edwardes signed up Fred Leslie, a talented light comedian, a fine singer and dancer and a superb mimic. Leslie was almost young enough to be Nellie Farren's son, but he adapted his style to suit her personality and they swiftly developed into an

10. George Edwardes launched musical comedies at the Gaiety in the 'nineties and became the leading producer of musical plays at the Gaiety, Daly's and elsewhere in the Edwardian era.

outstanding combination. Fred Leslie played villainous Jonathan Wild, the thief taker, Jack Shepherd's deadly enemy, with such grotesque humour that the audience were soon eating out of his hand. Edwardes persuaded Hollingshead to spend more money than usual on *Little Jack Shepherd*. Colourful sets replaced the utility scenery that

Hollingshead had been using in his last productions, and the chorus girls wore charming frocks and discarded their old tights forever.

Little Jack Shepherd, which opened on December 26, 1885, as a Christmas attraction, got splendid notices. 'It cannot be needful to say how the favourite [Nellie Farren] was received by a Boxing Day audience... There was heartiness in every cheer and enjoyment in every laugh raised by Miss Farren's well-remembered tricks of voice and manner', said one critic. After an excellent run at the Gaiety, *Little Jack Shepherd* toured the provinces with Nellie Farren and Fred Leslie, then it went out on a very profitable tour of Australia.

This new-style burlesque piece gave the partnership of Edwardes and Hollingshead a flying start, and encouraged Edwardes to suggest they should put on something completely different next. *Dorothy* was a light comic opera, which took place in a Kent village in the middle of the eighteenth century. Dorothy, the squire's daughter, and her best friend, Lydia, masquerade as village girls at a hop festival and are wooed by Wilder and Sherwood, two gay bucks from town. Wilder, the squire's nephew, is on his way to call on him to try and get the old man to clear his debts. Dorothy and Lydia give the men their rings on the understanding they will prove faithful to their 'true village loves'. But at the squire's home Wilder and Sherwood fail to recognise Dorothy and Lydia and they flirt with the wrong girls, resulting in Dorothy extracting Lydia's ring from Sherwood and vice versa. Then Wilder and Sherwood, to pay off Wilder's debt to the sheriff's officer, fake an attack on the squire and steal his money. After Dorothy and Lydia (disguised as men) challenge Wilder and Sherwood to a duel for the honour of the 'village girls', the squire turns up and the two couples pair off happily.

George Edwardes thought *Dorothy* would appeal to the same middle class audiences who had patronized Gilbert and Sullivan operas, but Hollingshead disagreed, declaring the piece too tame and sugary for the Gaiety patrons and not clever enough for the Savoy ones. But Edwardes had such a strong hunch about *Dorothy* that he was prepared to produce it on his own; 'Honest John' wished him luck and washed his hands of the venture. Alfred Cellier, who had composed the score of *Dorothy,* had been the original conductor of

Gilbert and Sullivan and Edwardes knew him very well. Cellier's unused music for *Nell Gwynne* had been cleverly worked into a new libretto by B.C. Stephenson, the playwright.

Edwardes and his wife, Julia, had settled down in a big house at Park Square West, Regent's Park. When he began rehearsing *Dorothy,* he grew so excited about the piece that he couldn't stop talking about it when he got home from the theatre. Julia's first child was a girl, so it was inevitable that she was christened Dorothy. He had given the key role of Dorothy to Marion Hood, the beautiful actress who had made her name singing 'Poor Wandering One' in *The Pirates of Penzance.* The leading men were Redfern Hollins and Hayden Coffin, a handsome actor with a fine singing voice. The sheriff's officer, Lurcher, was played by Arthur Williams, one of the Gaiety's best burlesque comedians. As the first night approached George Edwardes began to worry that Marion Hood's voice might be too weak for her solo numbers. But, feeling that it was too late to think of engaging another actress, he gambled on her being all right on the night.

Dorothy opened at the Gaiety on September 25, 1886, and had a poor reception. Marion Hood was very nervous and never got under the skin of her part, and failed in her solos. Redfern Hollins as Wilder, the hero, was another weak spot. In any case, it seemed that Hollingshead had been right and the Gaiety was the wrong theatre for the piece. The *Daily Telegraph* started by applauding Alfred Cellier's music: '... amid the fun and frolic the hand of a skilled musician is manifest. The composer does not stand forth simply as a melody maker, with just enough skill to dress up his tunes decently ... Not often perhaps has a comic opera been heard with more satisfaction than in this case ... There is scarcely a number which does not rise above the common order.'

Then the critic turned his attention to the performance of Marion Hood: 'She should be less fussy, much less conscious of herself and the audience, and free from the mannerisms which tire when they do not annoy.' He went on to say that Redfern Hollins, as Wilder, sang far better than he acted in the piece. But, 'Mr Hayden Coffin [Sherwood] is excellent both as an actor and singer and might with advantage have more to do.'

When George Edwardes presented a piece he used to concentrate on studying the audience on the first night. At *Dorothy* he had turned his back on the stage and watched the audience's reactions. A few days after the opening he called in B.C. Stephenson and had the piece reconstructed. He decided to let Marion Hood keep her part, hoping that she would improve in it. He thought Hayden Coffin should be given a special solo, and eventually an old number by Alfred Cellier was found at Chappell; Stephenson wrote a new lyric to it and called it 'Queen of my Heart'. Hayden Coffin sang it as a serenade to Dorothy outside her bedroom.

The first time Hayden Coffin sang 'Queen of my Heart' he was encored seven times; its rather 'daring' romantic sentiment appealed immensely to the audience:

I stand at your threshold sighing
As the cruel hours creep by,
And the time is slowly dying
That once too quickly did fly.
Your beauty o'er my being
Has cast a subtle spell.
And alas there is no fleeing
From the charms you wield so well.
For my heart is wildly beating
As it never beat before.
One word! one whispered greeting
In mercy I implore.

For from daylight a hint we must borrow
And prudence might come with the light!
Then why should we wait till to-morrow?
You are Queen of my Heart to-night.

Although Hayden Coffin was invariably encored when he sang 'Queen of my Heart' at the Gaiety, the house remained half empty. Feeling that *Dorothy* was a hopeless proposition at the Gaiety, George Edwardes transferred it to the Prince of Wales's, a smaller theatre. Henry J. Leslie, his assistant producer, had already told him he thought Marion Hood was the wrong actress for Dorothy, but Edwardes still refused to sack her, perhaps because he was a soft-hearted man who hated getting rid of an artiste in his company.

Dorothy fared no better at the Prince of Wales's. Towards the end of the year Gilbert and Sullivan began rehearsals of *Ruddigore* at the Savoy. George Edwardes happened to meet George Grossmith and Rutland Barrington, both of whom assured him that *Ruddigore* was going to be the biggest success of all the Gilbert and Sullivan operas. Edwardes believed them and, convinced that *Dorothy* could never compete with *Ruddigore* when it came on in the New Year, he decided to cut his losses and sold the piece lock, stock and barrel to Henry Leslie for £1,000.

Henry Leslie sacked Marion Hood and engaged a lesser known actress to play Dorothy; her name was Marie Tempest. Though not beautiful, Marie Tempest had the voice of a prima donna, a great stage presence and a gift for comedy. Leslie also sacked Redfern Hollins and brought in Ben Davies to play the role of Wilder. He retained Hayden Coffin as Sherwood and Arthur Williams continued in his old comedy part of Lurcher, the sheriff's officer.

While *The Mikado* was still on, W.S. Gilbert had picked a quarrel with D'Oyly Carte. He wrote Carte a letter which implied that he behaved like a dictator at the Savoy, and went on to propose that the management of the theatre should in future be divided between Carte, Sullivan and himself. This proposal infuriated Carte, who replied: 'It seems to me we are not all of the same opinion as to our respective positions under the contract . . . I cannot see how you and Sullivan are part managers of the theatre, any more than I am part author or part composer of the music . . .'

Carte's letter might have sounded reasonable to most people, but it threw Gilbert into a rage. He replied on June 11, 1885: 'I am at a loss to express the pain and surprise with which I read your letter.' He accused Carte of 'declining to permit me any voice in the control of the theatre that Sullivan and I have raised to its present position of prosperity and distinction.' And he warned Carte that in future he would only abide by the absolute and literal terms of their agreement.

In his lucid reply, Carte pointed out that *he* stood the whole risk of losses on their productions, but he had such faith in Gilbert and Sullivan that he was quite prepared to take this risk. However, Carte's letter made little impression on Gilbert. The trouble was that no power on earth could have altered his conviction that D'Oyly Carte, as their manager, was making too much money out of Gilbert and Sullivan's brains!

To follow *The Mikado* Gilbert had written *Ruddygore* – its original title – a parody of the tuppence coloured melodramas of the period. Its hero is haunted by his evil ancestors who try and force him to do a wicked deed every day of his life. When Sullivan first saw the libretto he was immensely pleased as it gave him much more scope to write music of his own instead of the usual procedure of simply setting Gilbert's lyrics to music. (In fact *Ruddigore* probably contains some of the finest music Sullivan ever composed for a comic opera.)

This was in January 1886 when Sullivan had already promised to write his *Golden Legend* for the Leeds Festival. Sullivan concentrated on *The Golden Legend* with the result that on April 3 Gilbert attacked him for his delay in setting their new piece, which was due for production in the autumn. It was particularly unfortunate that at this time the Prince of Wales asked him to set an Ode by Tennyson as a hymn for the Colonial and Indian Exhibition. This was a request that Sir Arthur Sullivan couldn't possibly refuse. He confided to his diary: 'How am I going to get through this year's work? ... Do they think me a barrel organ? they turn a handle and I disgorge music of any mood to order...'

The Golden Legend, with a libretto by Joseph Bennett based on Longfellow's poem, had a great triumph at Leeds, and in December Sullivan conducted performances of his oratorio at the Albert Hall and the Crystal Palace. *Ruddygore* was postponed till the following January; even then the score kept Sullivan feverishly busy and he often worked on it in January till 5:00 in the morning. It was finished on the 13th, only eight days before the first night.

George Grossmith had been cast as Robin Oakapple, the rather conventional hero, a part which gave him less opportunities than usual for exploiting his genius for comedy. Gilbert gave Jessie Bond the extremely difficult role of Mad Margaret; her wonderful performance surprised Gilbert and Sullivan and everyone connected with the Savoy. Rutland Barrington played Sir Despard Murgatroyd, the wicked baronet who reforms in the second act and leads Mad Margaret to the altar. Jessie Bond and Rutland Barrington had developed into a magnificent acting team. A great rapport had grown up between them; it only needed a certain inflection in Barrington's voice for Jessie to give the reaction he wanted, and she only had to lift an eyebrow for Barrington to know exactly what she expected him to do next.

In order to recoup his losses on *Dorothy,* George Edwardes put on burlesque pieces again at the Gaiety. As he prepared to produce Nellie Farren and Fred Leslie in *Monte Cristo, Junior,* a crisis blew up at the theatre because John Hollingshead had collapsed with a serious attack of rheumatic fever and could no longer attend to business. Hollingshead had invested in a speculative business in Manchester, which failed suddenly, putting him on the verge of bankruptcy. 'Honest John' then offered Edwardes his half share of the Gaiety at a very fair price. It was the opportunity of a lifetime for Edwardes, but he couldn't find the money owing to the failure of *Dorothy.* However, he managed to overcome the difficulty by going to Grimsby and calling on some of his old school friends in the fishing trade. They were making money hand over fist and jumped at the idea of investing some of their profits with George Edwardes for a share of the Gaiety Theatre. Edwardes went back to John Hollingshead and clinched the deal, which made him Guv'nor of the Gaiety at the age of thirty.

Monte Cristo, Junior was, of course, a skit on the famous Dumas novel. Nellie Farren impersonated the intrepid hero, Edmond Dantes, and Fred Leslie appeared as Nortier, the villainous attorney, indulging in such grotesque antics that he had the audience in stitches on December 23, 1886. The *Era* said: 'We couple the names of Miss Farren and Mr Leslie together because they are inseparable on stage, where they play into each other's hands as only two such artistes can.'

Monte Cristo, Junior did extremely well, and Edwardes presented a second edition in 1887. Afterwards Nellie Farren and Fred Leslie toured the provinces, then went off on very successful tours of Australia and America. The new Guv'nor had retrieved the situation at the Gaiety, and he knew that, so long as his two stars could carry on playing there, he could count on filling the house. But in spite of the setback with *Dorothy,* George Edwardes refused to abandon his idea of producing musical plays which would one day give Gilbert and Sullivan a run for their money.

PART 3
The Guv'nor calls the tune

CHAPTER EIGHT

DOROTHY UPSETS THE APPLECART

Why in the world we are to throw up the sponge and begin all over again because *Dorothy* has run 500 performances beats my comprehension.

W.S. GILBERT LETTER TO ARTHUR SULLIVAN, 1888

The first night of *Ruddygore* on January 22, 1887, was almost a disaster for the Savoy triumvirate; the gallery booed it at the end, and somebody shouted 'Take it away – give us back *The Mikado*!' The first act had gone very well, but in the last 20 minutes the melodramatic situation of Robin Oakapple being forced to do a wicked deed every day was suddenly stood on its head by Robin refusing to commit any more crimes and thus being sentenced to death, which would be suicide – another crime. The audience felt cheated by this melodrama and infinitely preferred the Gilbert of old. Apart from that, there had been a catastrophe when the family ghosts stepped out of their frames in the picture gallery and, through incompetent stage management, two of the family portraits crashed down on the stage.

'Shortly after the beginning of the second act the interest of the story begins to flag, until at last the plot had seemed within an inch of collapsing,' said the *St James's Gazette*. Sullivan was more upset than anybody by this reception, having written some notable music in his score. His best number, 'The Ghosts' High Noon', was sung by Sir Roderick Murgatroyd after he steps out of his frame:

When the night wind howls in the chimney cowls, and the
bat in the moonlight flies,
And inky clouds, like funeral shrouds, sail over the midnight
skies –
When the footpads quail at the night-bird's wail, and black
dogs bay the moon,
Then is the spectres' holiday – this is the ghosts' high noon!

And the sob of the breeze sweeps over the trees and the
mists lie low on the fen,
From grey tomb-stones are gathered the bones that once
were women and men,
And away they go, with a mop and a mow, to the revel that
ends too soon,
For cock crow limits our holiday – the dead of the night's
high noon!

The day after *Ruddygore's* poor reception, Gilbert and Sullivan
called a special meeting of the whole company; Gilbert made several
cuts in the piece and, as there had been complaints about the blood-
thirsty title, he agreed to alter a single letter and changed it to
Ruddigore. Some people felt he had overstepped the mark by pairing
off Dame Hannah with the ghost of her old suitor, Sir Roderick
Murgatroyd – and Gilbert cut dialogue from their scene. In May
Geraldine Ulmar, an American actress who had sung in the Savoy
operas in America, took over the role of Rose Maybud from Leonora
Braham. The *Era* reported:

From the first the Savoy has been nightly crowded. All the drawbacks attending the
first night were speedily overcome and we have seldom seen a more finished and
complete rendering of a comic opera... A performer in Messrs Gilbert and
Sullivan's operas must not only be a clever vocalist but must also possess that
somewhat rare feminine qualification – the gift of humourous expression. Miss
Ulmar is especially fortunate in this respect. Her archness and vivacity, her quiet,
unforced drollery of manner and a quaintness characteristic of American humour
generally... made it evident before Miss Ulmar had been many minutes on the
stage that her success was certain. Her bright, intelligent face and the rapidity with
which she could change its expression, enabled her to give the fullest effect to the
whimsicalities of the character.

However, the various cuts and modifications made little difference to
the fate of *Ruddigore.* Business began to drop as the piece lost favour
with the public; it was withdrawn after 298 performances, making it a
failure by Gilbert and Sullivan's standards.

Dorothy, with Marie Tempest in the name part, was presented by
Henry Leslie at the Prince of Wales's on February 19, 1887. The *Daily*

11. Alfred Cellier, who conducted the first Gilbert and Sullivan operas, also composed several comic operas including *Dorothy,* which ran longer than *The Mikado* with Marie Tempest in the leading role.

Telegraph said, 'Miss Marie Tempest enters thoroughly into the spirit of the character she presents, making it attractive in all dramatic respects and investing the music with the charm of good singing. Her success with Saturday night's audience was never in doubt... Mr Ben Davies gave special distinction to the tenor solos and through his excellent voice and spirited singing... There can scarecely be a doubt that *Dorothy* – one of the cleverest and most agreeable works of its kind – has now entered upon a new lease of popularity . . .'

Dorothy became the hit of the season; Hayden Coffin was encored every night for his song 'Queen of my Heart', which became the most popular ballad of the day. The piece did such phenomenal business that from its profits Henry Leslie built a new theatre in Shaftesbury Avenue which he called the Lyric; *Dorothy* was transferred to the Lyric as soon as it was ready. George Edwardes felt perfectly miserable at having missed the boat with this piece; for a long time he couldn't bear to hear the very name Dorothy, and as his eldest daughter had been called Dorothy it only rubbed salt in his wounds. Alfred Cellier, composer of *Dorothy*, had no idea of its extraordinary success because he was at the other end of the world in Australia, where he had gone in the hope of curing his consumption. The first inkling he had of *Dorothy's* triumph was when he received a huge cheque one morning from the sales of 'Queen of my Heart'.

The success of *Dorothy* plunged Sir Arthur Sullivan into the depths of despair; he felt that if Cellier's piece was what the public really wanted to see, then there was no future for the high quality Savoy operas, whose scores had caused him so much sweat and tears. After *Ruddigore* had come off, Sullivan wrote to Gilbert, who was plotting out their next piece, in a defeatist mood. He stated he had lost heart in their enterprise and felt it was not worth wrecking his health by writing any more Savoy operas when a fairly ordinary comic opera like *Dorothy* could break records.

His letter made Gilbert extremely angry, particularly as he was hard at work on their new piece, and thoroughly enjoying himself. Hoping to convince Sullivan that *Dorothy* must never be allowed to end their partnership, he wrote: 'Why in the world we are to throw up the sponge and begin all over again because *Dorothy* has run 500 performances beats my comprehension. We have the best theatre, the best company, the best composer, and (though I say it) the best librettist in England working together – we are well known and as much an institution as Westminster Abbey – and to scatter this splendid organization because *Dorothy* has run 500 nights is, to my way of thinking, to give up a gold mine. What is *Dorothy's* success to us? ... Is no piece but ours to run 500 or 600 nights? Did other companies dissolve because *Mikado* ran 650 nights?'

Gilbert's hard hitting letter had just the effect he had hoped for. Sullivan came to his senses and saw the *Dorothy* phenomenon in its true perspective. His thoughts returned to Gilbert's new libretto; he had already noted in his diary: 'Gilbert read plot of new piece [*Tower of London*]; immensely pleased with it, pretty story, no topsy-turvydom, very human and funny also.'

The new comic opera took place in the Tower of London in Tudor times; the first lyrics soon reached Sullivan and he began setting them to music. Gilbert, a disciplined playwright, used to sit up writing at his desk all through the night till the early hours of the morning. Sullivan, on the other hand, found it almost impossible to work at regular hours. He never minded if his nephew, Herbert, interrupted him while he was composing, and used to allow special friends to come in and see him if they called at his flat. When working he used to smoke countless cigarettes from a long amber holder. He first decided what kind of rhythm he was going to use for a number, then drafted out a sketch of it in his musical shorthand, and wrote the vocal parts afterwards. The Savoy company used to rehearse the vocal parts of his scores with only a piano accompanying them, and afterwards Sullivan would complete the orchestrations.

D'Oyly Carte's first wife had died in 1885 after a long illness. He married Helen Lenoir quietly at the Savoy Chapel in 1888, their best man being Sir Arthur Sullivan. It has been said with good reason that no theatre manager had ever been lucky enough to marry such a wonderful helpmeet as Helen D'Oyly Carte was to her husband. The new Gilbert and Sullivan opera was to become known as *The Yeomen of the Guard*. Sullivan again delivered his score late because of his commitments to conduct orchestras at several music festivals, and his very busy social life. Since *The Yeomen of the Guard* was due to open on October 3, Gilbert began to rehearse it in the first week of September before Sullivan had completed the whole score. When Sullivan had finished his last numbers, he had a feeling that this dramatic story which took place in the Tower of London would be their masterpiece, and Gilbert agreed with him.

Arthur Sullivan had had to call on Gilbert after he had spent weeks trying to devise the right setting for Jack Point's number, 'I have a song to sing–O'. He told Gilbert: 'You often have some old air in your mind which prompts the metre of your songs. If anything prompted you in this one, hum it to me – it may help me.' Gilbert remembered a sea shanty which the sailors on his yacht used to sing in the dog-watch on Saturday evenings. He hummed a few bars of it and Sullivan shouted: 'That will do – I've got it!' He ran to the piano and composed 'I have a song to sing–O', the key number in the piece, in an hour.

On the first night of *The Yeomen of the Guard* on October 3, 1888, Gilbert was a bundle of nerves. Instead of starting with an opening chorus as usual, the curtain went up on Jessie Bond (Phoebe Meryll) alone on the stage at her spinning wheel, singing 'When Maiden Loves'. Gilbert suddenly got panicky in case the audience were put off by Phoebe opening the piece. During the Overture he hovered round Jessie Bond on the stage and kept saying, 'Is everything right, Jessie?' She told him it was and off he went, but he was back again in a few seconds. 'Are you *sure* you're all right, Jessie?' he repeated. 'Yes, yes', she stammered, anxious only to be left alone. 'I'm *quite* all right.' Then he kissed her, danced around the stage in a kind of panicky excitement, and vanished again. But once more he came in, and there were more kisses, more dancing, and more inquiries. By this time the orchestra had nearly finished the overture. Jessie Bond couldn't stand his fussing any longer, and blurted out: 'For Heaven's sake, Mr Gilbert, go away and leave me alone or I shan't be able to sing a note!'

Jessie Bond kept her head and gave a superb performance as Phoebe Meryll, who is in love with Colonel Fairfax, the prisoner in the Tower, but forced to promise to marry the odious head jailer to secure his silence about her part in Fairfax's escape. George Grossmith, a comedian, had a challenging role as Jack Point, the tragi-comic jester. His sweetheart, Elsie Maynard, was admirably played by Geraldine Ulmar, and Colonel Fairfax was acted and sung with great distinction by Courtice Pounds.

Sir Arthur Sullivan's diary of the first night said: 'I was awfully nervous and continued so until the duet 'Heighday'[1] which settled the fate of the opera. Its success was tremendous... After that, everything went on wheels, and I think its success is even greater than *The Mikado*'.

The Yeomen of the Guard received some outstandingly good notices. 'Sir Arthur Sullivan has never written anything more delicately melodious and elegant', said the *Morning Advertiser,* writing of 'I have a song to sing-O'. 'Mr Gilbert is a man of genius, and even at his worst is head and shoulders above the ordinary librettist', said the *Times.* The *Daily Telegraph* critic wrote: 'We place the songs and choruses of *The Yeomen of the Guard* before all his previous efforts of this particular kind. Thus the music follows the book to a higher plane, and we have the genuine English opera, forerunner of many others, let us hope.'

However, some critics considered the plot too heavy for a Savoy opera. Colonel Fairfax has been unjustly condemned to be beheaded at the Tower; the day before his execution he makes a marriage of convenience with Elsie Maynard, Jack Point's sweetheart and partner. But then Phoebe Meryll, who has fallen in love with Fairfax, steals the chief jailer's keys enabling Fairfax to escape from his cell. Fairfax and Elsie fall in love, and when he is pardoned they rejoice in the fact that they are already married. When Jack Point learns that Elsie is leaving him for ever, the broken-hearted jester falls dead at her feet.

Outstanding numbers in the piece included 'Is Life a Boon?', 'Strange Adventure', 'Were I thy Bride' and 'The screw may twist and the rack may turn'. 'I have a song to sing-O' seems to haunt every scene in *The Yeomen of the Guard*; it is a rare song that many people remember all their lives:

I have a song to sing-O
It is sung to the moon
By a love-lorn loon,
Who fled from the mocking throng-O!
It's the song of the merryman moping mum,
Whose soul was sad, and whose glance was glum,

[1]Sullivan is referring to 'I have a song to sing-O', sung first as a duet by Jack Point and Elsie Maynard.

Who sipped no sup, and craved no crumb
And sighed for the love of a ladye.
Heighdy! heighdy!
Misery me, lackadayee!
He sipped no sup, and he crave no crumb,
As he sighed for the love of a ladye.

Like Gilbert and Sullivan, D'Oyly Carte believed that *The Yeoman of the Guard* would surpass the box office success of *The Mikado*. But the public decided the piece was too serious and thought the Tower of London made too sombre a setting for a comic opera, while Gilbert's jokes about racks and thumbscrews were considered in very poor taste. For a year *The Yeomen of the Guard* did excellent business, then the receipts went right down. Sullivan took this disappointment very badly; he grew restless and felt it was time to sever his connection with the Savoy operas. For a long time he had resented having to wait until Gilbert had written his libretto and sent him some lyrics before he could start to compose the score.

Sir Arthur Sullivan had recently conducted his oratorio, *The Golden Legend*, at a Royal Command performance at the Albert Hall. Queen Victoria had said to him afterwards, 'You ought to write a grand opera, Sir Arthur, you would do it so well.' To a born courtier like Sullivan, a hint from the Queen was as good as a Royal command for him to write a grand opera. He became obsessed with the idea of composing a grand opera which would establish his reputation once and for all as a major composer. One of the things about grand opera that particularly appealed to him was that, as the composer, he would be the master in the enterprise and the librettist would be subordinate to him – the opposite of the present position in which he had to play second fiddle to W.S. Gilbert.

Gilbert's temper had worsened on account of his gout; rehearsals of *The Yeomen of the Guard* took place in an unpleasant atmosphere, and Gilbert and Sullivan had several rows, causing the composer to write in his diary; 'I can't stand it any longer.'

Sullivan had noticed a lack of enthusiasm for one of his numbers the first time he played it to the company. He asked Gilbert if anything was the matter, and was told: 'My dear fellow, I know nothing about music. I can't tell the difference between 'Rule Britannia' and 'Pop Goes the Weasel'. I merely know there is a composition and decomposition – in other words rot – and that's what your tune is!'

Sullivan wrote to D'Oyly Carte in 1889 in a desperate strain, complaining that Gilbert had been overbearing and impossible to work with at rehearsals of *The Yeomen*. He continued: 'I am only a cipher in the theatre... They are Gilbert's pieces with music added by me. You can hardly wonder that twelve years of this has a little tired me, and unless a change in the construction of the piece and in the manner of rehearsing and producing it is made, I would wish to give up altogether... You had better bring the substance of this letter to Gilbert.'

Sullivan was a complex character; only the previous day he had written a letter to Gilbert in a much more conciliatory tone. One assumes that Sullivan, who had a timid streak in his nature, was afraid of airing his grievances direct to Gilbert, preferring to act through Carte. The latter was certainly not in awe of the formidable Gilbert; when he showed him Sullivan's letter, Gilbert nearly hit the roof. Carte, well aware of how much the Savoy depended on Gilbert and Sullivan operas, exerted all his diplomacy to persuade the partners to make up their differences. Eventually, Gilbert graciously assured Sullivan that in future he would make every effort to see that they worked together as 'master' and 'master'.

But then Gilbert nearly spoilt everything by sending Sullivan a preliminary outline for their next piece, which was nothing more than a camouflaged version of his 'lozenge' plot. Sullivan turned it down again and Gilbert left him, feeling disappointed. But a few days later he wrote to say that Venice had inspired him to write a comic opera. Sullivan was so relieved to hear that the 'lozenge' plot had been abandoned that he accepted the new story without a quibble. If he had looked a little closer at the skeleton of *The Gondoliers,* he would have discovered that Gilbert had returned to his topsy-turvy manner.

CHAPTER NINE

THE FATAL QUARREL

Sullivan is the sort of man who will sit on a fire and then complain that
his bottom is burning.

W.S. GILBERT

When *The Gondoliers* was presented on December 7, 1889, the public
welcomed the return of Rutland Barrington to the Savoy and gave
him a tremendous cheer on his first appearance as Guiseppe, one of
the gondoliers. Gilbert and Sullivan had returned to their topsy-turvy
manner and the audience applauded them to the last note. This comic
opera is the story of Marco and Guiseppe, two gondoliers who have
been mixed up at birth. One of them is the heir to the throne of
Barataria, a small country near Venice, but nobody knows which of
them it is; so the goldoliers leave their brides to go and rule jointly
over a utopian kingdom where everybody is equal and class has been
abolished.

George Grossmith had left the company because he was getting
Gilbert had tremendous fun standing the egalitarian ideal on its
head; he wrote a flawless libretto to which Sullivan composed a witty
and enchanting score. The press endorsed the first nighters; *Punch*
was moved to say, 'The piece is so brilliant to the eye and ear that
there is never a dull moment on the stage or off it.' *The Illustrated
London News* summed up the general opinion: 'Mr W.S. Gilbert has
returned to the Gilbert of the past, and everyone is delighted. He is
himself again . . . the Gilbert who on Saturday night was cheered till
the audience grew weary of cheering any more.'

George Grossmith had left the company because he was getting
on in years and finding the effort of gallivanting about the Savoy stage
too much for him. He also wanted to get away from Gilbert's
domineering methods as a producer and return to the comfortable
routine of being a concert entertainer. Gilbert, taking a leaf from the
egalitarian theme of *The Gondoliers*, had written nine principal parts

of more or less equal importance. 'Take a pair of sparkling eyes', sung by Courtice Pounds as Marco, the second goldolier, is one of the gems of the Savoy operas:

Take a pair of sparkling eyes,
Hidden, ever and anon,
In a merciful eclipse –
Do not heed their mild surprise,
Having crossed the Rubicon.
Take a pair of rosy lips;
Take a figure trimly planned –
Such as admiration whets
(Be particular in this):
Take a tender little hand
Fringed with dainty fingerettes,
Press it – in parenthesis –
Take all these, you lucky man
Take and keep them, if you can!

W.H. Denny as Don Alhambra, the Grand Inquisitor, was encored for his number. 'There lived a king', which relates what happens when everybody is promoted to the top of the tree:

Lord Chancellors were cheap as sprats,
And Bishops in their shovel hats
Were plentiful as tabby cats –
In point of fact, too many.
Ambassadors cropped up like hay
Prime Ministers and such as they
Grew like asparagus in May,
And Dukes were two a penny!
On every side Field Marshals gleamed,
With Admirals the ocean teemed
All round his wide dominions.
And Party leaders you might meet
In twos and threes in every street,
Maintaining with no little heat,
Their various opinions.

Sullivan admitted in an interview that *The Gondoliers* had been more trouble to compose than any of his previous pieces. Owing to the fast tempo of the music it is the longest score in the Gilbert and Sullivan canon, and it had cost Sullivan a great effort to sustain the brilliance of the music throughout this comic opera. His health had started to break up under the strain of forcing himself to work at all hours while in great pain.

The day after *The Gondoliers* opened, Gilbert wrote to Sullivan: 'I must thank you again for the magnificent work you have put into the piece. It gives me the chance of shining through the twentieth century with a reflected light.' Sullivan replied generously: 'Don't talk of reflected light. In such a perfect book as *The Gondoliers* you shine with an individual brilliancy which no other writer can hope to attain. If any thanks are due anywhere, they should be from me to you for the patience, willingness, and unfailing good nature with which you have received my suggestions and your readiness to help me by acceding to them.'

It really sounded as if the composer and librettist had formed a mutual admiration society and would henceforth never exchange a cross word during their partnership. People queued up for hours to book seats for *The Gondoliers*; D'Oyly Carte had known nothing like it since the halcyon days of *The Mikado*. *The Gondoliers* ran for 550 performances, its success in England and abroad matching that of *The Mikado*.

Under such circumstances, one can only marvel that Gilbert should have chosen to pick a quarrel with Carte in 1890 which struck a mortal blow at the triumvirate. Sullivan had left England to take a much needed holiday in the South of France, intending to stay there as long as possible before returning to start work on his grand opera, *Ivanhoe*. Gilbert wrote him a letter out of the blue which almost ruined his holiday!

> 39 Harrington Gardens,
> S. Kensington.
> 22nd April, 1890.

My dear Sullivan,

MR. BARRINGTON & MISS JESSIE BOND in "RUDDIGORE."

COPYRIGHT.

Barraud, 263, Oxford St London.

12. Rutland Barrington as the reformed Sir Despard Murgatroyed and Mad Margaret (Jessie Bond) have just become Sunday school teachers in *Ruddigore*, produced at the Savoy in 1887. Although it failed by Gilbert and Sullivan's standards, it brought Gilbert £7,000 in royalties.

I've had a difficulty with Carte.

I was appalled to learn from him that the preliminary expenses of *The Gondoliers,* amounted to the stupendous total of £4,500!! This seemed so utterly unaccountable that I asked to see the details, and last night I received a resumé of them . . . But the most surprising item was *£500 for new carpets for the front of the house!*

(Gilbert said he had protested to Carte that these preliminary expenses were too high, and that he ought to make some adjustments in the accounts. The letter continued:)

He replied that the only alteration he would agree to would be to put the rent of the theatre at £5,000 instead of the £4,000 and that if I was dissatisfied with the existing state of affairs I had only to say so. I replied that I *was* dissatisfied and he said, 'Very well, then; you write no more for the Savoy – that's understood' – or words to that effect. I left him with the remark that it was a mistake to kick down the ladder by which he had risen . . .

I am sorry to bother you with this long letter, but I am sure you will agree with me that it is absolutely necessary that a distinct understanding should be arrived at, if we are to work for Carte again.

Always truly yours,
W.S. Gilbert.

Gilbert's letter protesting about the charge for new carpets at the Savoy put Sullivan in a most embarrassing position: not only were he and D'Oyly Carte great friends, but Carte had specially arranged to produce his grand opera, *Ivanhoe,* at his new Opera House. And in any case Sullivan felt Carte was quite justified in charging them for new carpets at the theatre. Arthur Sullivan had an easygoing nature, he hated rows and was not a fighter. Feeling that Gilbert was making a mountain out of a molehill, he refused to support him against Carte and quite expected that the affair would blow over. But when Gilbert

13. Rosina Brondram as the formidable Duchess of Plaza-Toro in *The Gondoliers*, 1889, the second most successful of all the Savoy operas.

learnt that Sullivan, his fellow artist, was siding with Carte, the businessman, in their dispute, he flew into one of his rages.

While Sullivan refused to be drawn into the quarrel, and was prepared to follow the advice of D'Oyly Carte who had told him, 'You stick to me', Gilbert went into battle. On May 5th, 1890, he wrote to Sullivan as follows:

> The time for putting an end to our collaboration has at last arrived . . . I am writing a letter to Carte (of which I enclose a copy) giving him notice that he is not to produce or perform any of my libretti after Christmas 1890. In point of fact, after the withdrawal of *The Gondoliers,* our united work will be heard in public no more.

Sullivan was ill and his overriding interest was to complete the score of *Ivanhoe*; he needed Carte to help him to realize his life's ambition with the production of his grand opera, and the last thing he wanted was having to go to all the trouble of studying the Savoy accounts. Carte, of course, had no sympathy with Gilbert, whom he regarded as a troublemaker. However, Carte took the initiative in this impasse and arranged for the triumvirate to meet and discuss the matter at his flat in Adelphi Terrace. But at this meeting neither Gilbert nor Carte would budge from their positions over the Savoy carpets.

A week later a 'peace conference' was held at the Savoy at which Helen D'Oyly Carte joined them. Gilbert had always had the greatest respect for her, and Carte was hoping he would behave reasonably in her presence. But unfortunately Gilbert lost his temper from the start and harped on his old grievance against Carte, saying 'I demand a fresh agreement because *you* are making too much money out of *my* brains!' Then he accused Carte in violent language of robbing Sullivan and himself right and left, declaring that Carte was so negligent that he didn't even check his carpenters' accounts! He shouted that Carte had forbidden him to write for the Savoy any more, but Helen Carte denied this. Finally, Gilbert called Carte and Sullivan a couple of blackguards, and stormed out of the meeting.

D'Oyly Carte wrote a dignified letter to Gilbert the following week, informing him that the cost of the new carpets for the front of the house was £140 and not £500, as he had claimed. Carte explained that the preliminary costs of *The Gondoliers* had been high partly because Gilbert, in his role of producer, had ordered costumes and materials in such a hurry that Carte was never sent a proper estimate. He also pointed out that it was normal practice to expect Gilbert and Sullivan, as partners in the Savoy, to pay their share of the costs of keeping the theatre in good order. Carte's letter continued: 'You asked what I had done for the share I have got of our very successful enterprise. I have devoted the greater part of my time and energies to it . . . I and my wife have worked loyally in your interests, our first thought has always been to give a performance satisfactory to you and Sullivan and that would be a credit to our management. We have thought more of this than of any money we would make . . .'

But no power on earth could stop Gilbert once he had set his mind on a course of action. He called in his solicitor and his accountant and instructed them to go through the Savoy Theatre accounts item by item, convinced that Carte had been overcharging Sullivan and himself. When he appealed to Sullivan for his support, he received the following reply:

July 16

My dear Gilbert,

. . . I have no grievance – no dispute, and I have raised no question which would justify me at this juncture stepping in with the demand that the Savoy accounts should be kept in a different manner.

. . . the deplorable step of calling in lawyer and accountant has rendered a satisfactory settlement almost impossible. My object now is to do nothing that will add fuel to the fire, and consequently I hold entirely aloof from taking part in this unhappy dispute . . .

Yours very truly,

Arthur Sullivan.

In August Helen D'Oyly Carte made an eleventh hour attempt to reach a settlement with W.S. Gilbert by inviting him to come and see her alone at Adelphi Terrace. Gilbert admitted at their meeting that he had lost his temper and said things in the heat of the moment that he now regretted. But it was too late to patch things up because he had already started an action against D'Oyly Carte for failing to produce the accounts of the Savoy Theatre for the second quarter of the year. Carte had held up the accounts on the advice of his solicitor, Mr Stanley, pending a settlement of the dispute with Gilbert over the carpets.

The case of *W.S. Gilbert v. Richard D'Oyly Carte* for a missing account of *The Gondoliers* and for his full share of the net profits for the second quarter was heard in the High Court of Justice on September 3, 1890. Gilbert also applied for the appointment of a Receiver of the takings of *The Gondoliers*. An agreement of 1883 laid down that each of the triumvirate should receive one third of the net profits of the comic operas after deducting £4,000 a year for the rent of the Savoy Theatre, also the necessary expenses of running the theatre. Payments were to be made to Gilbert and Sullivan for their own use every quarter. In view of the fact that Sir Arthur Sullivan considered that D'Oyly Carte was justified in charging for the carpets at the Savoy, the three partners had reached a deadlock.

Gilbert protested that he had only received £2,000 on account in July, although he had ascertained that *The Gondoliers* had grossed £20,000 in the second quarter. His contention was that he was entitled to £3,000 as his share and, under the circumstances, he was applying for a Receiver to take over the Savoy Theatre in order to protect his future earnings.

Carte opposed Gilbert's application for a Receiver, stating that during the last eleven years the Savoy operas had brought Gilbert a total sum of £70,000 from England and £2,000 from provincial and American productions. He made out a strong case against allowing any interference with the management of the Savoy as it would be very prejudicial to the interests of all parties. The action was settled by D'Oyly Carte agreeing to pay Gilbert an extra £1,000 for the last quarter, and also undertaking to render up to date accounts to Gilbert within three weeks. However, Mr Justice Lawrence ruled that it was not necessary to appoint a Receiver at the Savoy.

Gilbert's case was discussed all over London and even far beyond the British Isles. The general opinion was that Gilbert must have been almost mad to have gone to law against Carte, the brilliant impresario who had been instrumental in bringing a fortune into his coffers. But Gilbert had an extremely high code of honour, and his training in the Law had helped to account for him bringing this action. After the Court proceedings on September 3, Gilbert's solicitors examined the Savoy accounts and found a serious discrepancy amounting to about £1400. Gilbert therefore wrote promptly to Sullivan to ask for his support under these circumstances. The composer replied as follows:

8 Sept. 1890.

My dear Gilbert,

You will I am sure readily understand the difficulty I feel in answering your letter. My old personal regard for you as a friend pleads strongly to let the past five months be blotted out by our years of friendship. But I am only human, and I confess frankly that I am still smarting under a sense of the unjust and ungenerous treatment I have received at your hands.

...Don't think me exagerrating when I tell you that I am physically and mentally ill over this wretched business – I have not yet got over the shock of seeing our names coupled, not in brilliant collaboration over a work destined for worldwide celebrity, but in hostile antagonism over a few miserable pounds.

Sullivan's letter was just a shade too sanctimonious and full of self-pity. Of course he hated the idea of the triumvirate washing their dirty linen in public, but the truth was that he had determined to stick to Carte at all costs, and therefore felt quite prepared to ignore the error of £1,400 in the Savoy accounts. Gilbert, of course, felt just the opposite about it.

Breakespeare, Uxbridge.

9 Sept.

Dear Sullivan,

95

> ...I cannot help reminding you that if, *after the discovery of an error of £1,400 in four months' accounts,* Carte had consented to my examining the books of the past years... *no legal proceedings would have been taken...*

Gilbert then reproached Sullivan for never making it clear to him that he really intended to oppose Gilbert's motion in his writ. His letter continued:

> I telegraphed to my solicitor (from Carlsbad, where he had gone to try and cure his gout) to confine himself to an application for the money due to me; he replied that owing to the form of the action this was impractical; that I must apply for a Receivership or forgo everything.

> ...I acted as I did simply because (as you had declined to interfere) I had no alternative except to bow to Carte's refusal to let me examine the books which are as much mine as are the scenery, dresses and properties purchased out of the receipts, and to allow him to retain money long since due and constantly accruing which you know he has no more right to than my watch and chain...

> Yours sincerely,

> W.S.G.

The most damning revelation in the case was brought to light in October. Before that *The Era* had summed up the general opinion of the 'carpet quarrel' on September 13:

The enterprising prophet who would have predicted six months ago that Mr W.S. Gilbert and Mr R. D'Oyly Carte would have figured as opponents in a court of law would have been regarded as weak in the brain. But those who have watched the progress of the Gilbert and Sullivan operas... have had to deplore a disagreement between librettist and manager which culminated in the case which was heard by Mr Justice Lawrence on 3rd September.

We can hardly allow ourselves to think that the breach which has been created by the proceedings... can be easily healed. This is the more to be regretted as the history of the Gilbert and Sullivan operas is phenomenal, not only on account of the large sums of money which the able collaborators and their able manager have earned, but for the strange fact that two people have managed for fifteen years to work without serious disagreement with Mr W.S. Gilbert. That gentleman's gift of genius is accompanied by a full share of the irritability which has long been an acknowledged attribute of the poetic race...

It was mentioned in the course of the case last week that the receipts (of *The Gondoliers*) for three months only, exceeded £20,000! The golden flood has poured into the coffers of the manager, the librettist and the composer almost without a pause. It was understood that *The Gondoliers* was to be the last of the series under existing contracts...

The person most to be pitied is Sir Arthur Sullivan, who, himself the least quarrelsome of men, found himself obliged to appear by counsel in opposition to his old friend and fellow-labourer in the vineyard where the grapes have been so golden and the crop so rich.

Gilbert's solicitors discovered in the course of September that the affidavit sworn by D'Oyly Carte and Sullivan on September 3 to protect their interests and prevent the appointment of a Receiver was not valid. Gilbert pointed out the facts to Sullivan as clearly as he possibly could:

Graem's Dyke,
Harrow Weald.
14 Oct., '90.

Dear Sullivan,

In my affidavit I swore that I had authorised no legal expenses which had not yet been brought into account, and that I believed there were no such expenses outstanding except, perhaps, for matters of insignificant account.

You, on the other hand, swore not only that there were legal expenses but that that there were in particular legal expenses still outstanding in connection with an action that I had expressly authorized...

It now appears that the action particularly referred to as one which I had personally authorized and the expenses of which were still outstanding, was the action commenced against us by Miss Lilian Russell 8 years ago (in connection with the actress playing in *Princess Ida*). It further appears, from a letter just received from Mr Stanley's firm, that the expenses were paid and charged against the joint accounts no less than 5 years ago. It further appears, from the same letter, that the only legal expenses still outstanding at the time of making your affidavit was an insignificant sum of £46... for which I am neither legally or morally liable...

I am willing to believe that your affidavit (which, in effect, charges me with perjury) was made under an entire misconception... In view of the great importance attached by the Court to the statements on oath of a man in your distinguised position, I must ask you whether you are prepared to give me in writing a distinct retraction of the clause of your affidavit to which this letter refers, with permission to make such use thereof as may appear to me desirable.

Yours truly,

W.S.G.

During October Sullivan was completely immersed in his com-position of *Ivanhoe*, so there was a good reason for him to postpone replying to Gilbert's letter. No doubt he was advised by Carte to sit tight and do nothing in the matter. Carte was now planning a future in which he and Sullivan would be the sole partners in the Savoy enterprise on a fifty-fifty basis. Gilbert gave Sullivan a few months in which to finish the score of his grand opera before he returned to the attack. Sullivan had been working on *Ivanhoe* since May, but the carpet quarrel had upset him so much that it had slowed up his rate of progress. Julian Sturgess had based the libretto on Sir Walter Scott's famous novel which Sullivan considered an ideal subject for an opera with its English background.

He still found *Ivanhoe* an uphill task in the autumn, although Sturgess went out of his way to give him as much co-operation as possible. Sullivan, working at River House, Walton-on-Thames, could hardly ever settle down to a normal day on his score; after composing for a few hours he would go off for the rest of the day on a long walk or go for a row on the river. It took him months to finish the

14. Exterior of the impressive Royal English Opera House at Cambridge Circus, opened by D'Oyly Carte on January 31, 1891 with Sullivan's grand opera, *Ivanhoe*. It failed and lost so much money that Carte had to sell the theatre, which became the Palace music hall.

first act because he put it aside so often to compose parts of the second and third acts. He often tore up pages of music that were useless, then called in Sturgess to reconstruct the scene for him. He completed *Ivanhoe* on December 13, saying 'it has been seven months hard labour'.

There were nine scenes in the three acts of *Ivanhoe,* and each scene required a different set. However, D'Oyly Carte went ahead and mounted 'Sullivan's masterpiece' sumptuously and regardless of expense at the English Opera House, expecting *Ivanhoe* to run at least a year. He engaged a double cast to perform the opera on alternate nights, and installed an orchestra of over sixty musicians. He overdid the advance publicity, leading the public to expect a work in the same class as Mozart or Gounod.

On January 30, 1891, the day before the premiere of *Ivanhoe,* Gilbert wrote to Sullivan again about the affidavit. After reminding the composer that the legal expenses mentioned in it had been settled over 5 years ago, he continued:

... In a friendly letter to you I drew your attention to this admitted fact and, anxious as I am to believe that you had sworn your affidavit under the influence of misinformation, I gave you the opportunity of withdrawing... the statement to which I have referred. In the course of an evasive reply, you curtly forbade me to make any further reference to these legal proceedings under penalty of forfeiting your personal friendship...

Sullivan replied to him the next day.

31st Jan. 1891.

My dear Gilbert,

I thought that bygones were to be bygones, and that no further reference was to be made to any of the matter lately in dispute. But it is evidently not your intention to bury them, without exacting from me an admission which might be construed either as an apology or a retraction. Forgive me for saying that I can neither apologize nor retract... I have never alluded to your affidavits and never questioned the good faith upon which they were made – why should you question mine? You speak of my evasive reply to your letter. I thought my reply was pretty straight forward inasmuch as I gave you details of the matters upon which my affidavit was founded and refused, as I do now, to admit that I was wrong. Surely, my dear Gilbert, you can afford to let things rest as they are now, and let us forget the past. Let your presence at the theatre to-night be an intimation that you are as ready and willing as I am to think no more of what has happened, and to allow nothing to disturb our old friendship.

Yours sincerely,
Arthur Sullivan.

However, Sullivan's soft soap did not satisfy Gilbert, and he declined his two stalls for *Ivanhoe*. The opera had a most glamourous premiere before a distinguised audience which included the Prince and Princess of Wales and the Duke and Duchess of Edinburgh. The audience, who had come to the new theatre to see a masterpiece, witnessed a panorama of events: Robin Hood and his merry men played rustic games in the forest, and gallant Ivanhoe humiliated the Templar in the lists. One short scene followed another, with several long waits in between; apart from that, the opera suffered badly from lack of human interest. Sullivan's score was unable to sustain the dramatic passages of *Ivanhoe,* and a great deal of the music fell below the standard of grand opera. The intelligent minority in the audience realized, amid all the cheering at the end, that Sullivan and Sturgess had produced a failure.

Most of the critics had nothing but praise for *Ivanhoe,* although Bernard Shaw was moved to say in *The World*: 'It really does not do to spread butter on both sides of the bread.' Ben Davies (who had played the hero in *Dorothy*) gave a fine performance and sang splendidly in the title role; Miss Macintyre played Rebecca and triumphed in her solo, 'Lord of our Chosen Race'. The *Daily Telegraph* gave the opera a rave notice, which ended by reporting that the audience left 'and carried news of a brilliant success all over London'.

In a mood of euphoria, D'Oyly Carte convinced himself that *Ivanhoe* was going to be a world-beater. Gilbert wrote to Sullivan again the day after his grand opera had been launched.

18 Chesham Place, S.W.

Feb. 1st.

Dear Sullivan,

I am ... most anxious to believe that you made the statement as to costs under a misapprehension, and I ask for no more than your simple word to that effect. I only ask you to say that, if you had known what you now know, you would not have sworn as you then swore. If ... you are in doubt whether those costs have been paid you have only to look at your very carefully kept accounts of 5 years ago, and you will

101

then find that our third of these costs of *Russell v. Carte* were then charged against you. Carte will tell you that they had been paid... yet you refuse to admit that, in saying that they were still unpaid, you were acting under a misapprehension.

...As it is, I will meet you when and where you please, if you think that such a meeting would promote a better understanding.

Yours sincerely,

W.S.G.

However, wild horses would not drag an admission from Sullivan that he had sworn a false affidavit.

Feb. 4th 1891.

Dear Gilbert,

...We look at things from such different points of view that I fear neither will ever be able to convince the other. You assume that I am in possession of facts of which in reality I am absolutely ignorant, and as you decline to receive the verification which I was desirous of obtaining from the person most competent to give it (Mr Stanley, solicitor of the Savoy Theatre), I am afraid the matter must rest where it stands.

Yours very truly,

Arthur Sullivan.

Ivanhoe did very well at the English Opera House until its hundredth performance; then for some reason – perhaps because audiences had found it disappointing after all the fuss and passed the word to their friends – the public deserted *Ivanhoe* and business slumped disastrously. The production costs were so enormous that D'Oyly Carte had to cut his losses and withdraw the grand opera after only 155 performances. He put on two failures afterwards, and was then forced to sell his brand new theatre at a very modest price to

Augustus Harris, the Drury Lane manager, who converted it into the Palace Music Hall where he ran music hall turns. It was a castastrophic setback for D'Oyly Carte; but in addition to this he had to face a sea of troubles at the Savoy in the 'nineties.

Gilbert's final letter to Sullivan about the affidavit was devastating and never received an answer:

28 May 1891

Dear Sullivan,

... As a direct result of the action I commenced against Carte ... he has admitted an overcharge of nearly £1,000 in the electric lighting accounts alone. He also admits that there are other items charged ... which should not have been charged and he expresses his readiness to put these matters right as soon as *The Gondoliers* is withdrawn. As you will, I suppose, benefit considerably by this readjustment of accounts I thought it possible that you might wish to share with me the costs of the action by which it was brought about.

Yours truly,

W.S.G.

Gilbert soon found a new collaborator in Alfred Cellier, the composer of *Dorothy* and the original conductor of the Gilbert and Sullivan operas. Cellier, a tall man with a drooping moustache, was so flattered by Gilbert's invitation to set his libretto to music that he agreed to write the score of another version of the perennial 'lozenge' plot. Cellier had been an enthusiastic Bohemian in his younger days. He and George Grossmith had once shared a cab from one of Arthur Sullivan's late parties. To Grossmith's astonishment, Cellier asked to be dropped at a house in Park Lane at 3:30 in the morning – another party was only just beginning at that hour!

When Gilbert and Cellier began their collaboration on *The Mountebanks,* the composer was in very poor health owing to his lung disease. In the autumn Alfred Cellier had to go abroad to a warmer climate and asked Gilbert if he wished to accompany him. But

Gilbert stayed at home and had great difficulty in communicating with Cellier as he moved on from Italy to Egypt and then to Australia. Gilbert started rehearsals in November on the understanding that Cellier had practically finished the score. Gilbert wrote letters to Cellier complaining because no music had arrived. Cellier's wife replied: 'Alfred has been ill . . . he has always thought it an honour to collaborate with so distinguished and successful a librettist as you are.'

After three weeks rehearsing *The Mountebanks,* Gilbert had only received four choruses from Cellier and wrote him a stiff letter, concluding: '. . . I will not submit to being trifled with as I have been during the last week. You told me distinctly four weeks ago that the music was "practically finished".' Alfred Cellier was only 47, but it cost him every ounce of energy to finish his score in December. When he met his friend Cunningham Bridgeman at a little West End club one evening, Cellier was so exhausted that he fell upon a couch and succumbed to a painful fit of hysteria.

Alfred Cellier died suddenly on December 27, only a few days before the first night. He and Arthur Sullivan had been life-long friends ever since they had been at school together at the Chapel Royal. Sullivan, who was in Paris when he heard the tragic news, immediately wrote to Francois Cellier, Alfred's brother, who had taken over as the Savoy conductor:

Dear Frank,

I can hardly see the paper for the tears which are in my eyes at the dreadful news just sent by telegram.

Poor dear old Alfred! my old schoolfellow and friend! the most lovable creature in the world . . .

The Mountebanks, presented at the Lyric on January 4, 1892, was very well received. Clement Scott in the *Daily Telegraph* began his notice with a reference to Cellier's death: 'Amid the laughter and applause which greeted the new opera of Messrs Gilbert and Cellier last night, the thoughts of many of us gathered round a newly made grave. The loss of Alfred Cellier is a great misfortune . . . When Mr Gilbert brings his puppets on to the stage he makes them so exquisitely droll that we are concerned with nothing but the fun of the moment ... the melody runs throughout in an increasing and delightful stream ... Nothing more refined and delicate than the orchestration of *The Mountebanks* can be found in comic opera ...'

The Mountebanks takes place at a Sicilian inn where all the characters drink from a magic phial left there by an old alchemist. It changes all their natures in the second act, and everybody becomes what they are and not what they appear to be. Amongst the people at the inn are a gang of bandits and their brides, a troupe of mountebanks, and two villagers who impersonate nobility for the innkeeper's benefit. They are all relieved when they are disenchanted in the last act and return to their normal selves. *The Mountebanks* made a good evening's entertainment, but couldn't be compared with vintage Gilbert and Sullivan; it ran for 226 performances. Though Gilbert's brain was teeming with ideas for another comic opera, he knew he couldn't count on Sullivan setting his work to music.

It was six years since George Edwardes had become Guv'nor of the Gaiety. His new-style burlesques with Nellie Farren and Fred Leslie had been extremely successful; but in 1892 their notable partnership came to an abrupt end. First Nellie Farren had to retire from the stage on account of her chronic rheumatic condition and Fred Leslie opened alone in *Cinder-Ellen-up-too-late*. It had only been running a few weeks when Leslie collapsed in his dressing room after a performance and died a few days later from typhoid fever at the age of 37.

Edwardes, forced to fill a great void at the Gaiety, virtually invented a new form of light entertainment known as musical comedy. It was roughly a cross between the French operettas of Offenbach and Lecocq, Gilbert and Sullivan, and the Gaiety burlesques. The new shows had plots as thin as a wafer, a succession of song and dance numbers in which the chorus boys and girls usually appeared in the latest fashions, and in between numbers the comedians came on and gagged away as much as they liked.

In Town, the first musical comedy, starred Arthur Roberts, an expert in the art of gagging, and was presented by George Edwardes at the Prince of Wales's on October 15, 1892. Arthur Roberts played

Captain Coddington, the epitome of the man about town, wearing the last word in Saville Row suitings. The lyric of 'The man about Town' by Adrian Ross hit off the Victorian masher so wittily that it might have been written by W.S. Gilbert:

> I'm a terrible swell it is easy to tell
> From my dress and my general deportment:
> And I wish to declare that of qualities rare
> I've a large and varied assortment.
> I'm at dinners and balls and suppers and halls,
> I'm never at home for a minute.
> And a 'Tableau Vivant' would be sure to go wrong
> If they hadn't included me in it;
> For I'm the chief and the crown,
> Of the Johnnies who stroll up and down:
> The affable, chaffable, cynical, finical, typical Man about
> Town.

The pioneer musical comedy, *In Town,* was written by James Tanner and Adrian Ross with music by Osmond Carr. A complete novelty, it did such excellent business that the Guv'nor transferred it to the Gaiety. The success of *In Town* encouraged him to hope that musical comedies might establish themselves as a popular form of entertainment and take over from Gaiety burlesques. If he had guessed right, then he would make his theatre the premier house of musical comedy.

CHAPTER TEN

END OF A GOLDEN ERA

There is no doubt in my mind that what the public want now is simply
'fun' and little else.

D'OYLY CARTE'S LETTER TO
W.S. GILBERT, 1893

The Savoy had gone dark for the first time since its opening when *The
Goldoliers* came off in the spring of 1891. It was a serious state of
affairs for D'Oyly Carte, coming on top of his huge losses on *Ivanhoe*.
Sullivan had started work on a new comic opera with Sidney Grundy,
the playwright, but it was not nearly ready; so Carte arranged to
present *The Nautch Girl*, a comic opera composed by Edward
Solomon, one of Sullivan's principal rivals. Solomon had made his
reputation in the 'eighties as an operetta composer with *The Vicar of
Bray*, *Claude Duval*, and *The Red Hussar*, in which Marie Tempest
had starred. Though Solomon was a fine musician, he worked too fast
to do himself justice and his melodies had a way of sounding too much
like Sullivan's. He wrote excellent patter songs and generally composed a waltz at the end of his first acts.

Teddy Solomon was a brilliant pianist, a gift inherited from his
father, Charlie Solomon, who had tickled the ivories at various
London pubs in the early days of music hall. A Jew with an engaging
personality, Solomon was extremely attractive to women and he
certainly adored the opposite sex. He had a string of mistresses and at
least two wives according to the records. He had deserted his first
wife, Jane, and their baby daughter in London in 1875. He went off to
America with Lilian Russell, the actress who had starred in his
operetta, *Pocohontas*, ten years later and carelessly married her at the
Dutch Reformed Church at Hoboken although he had not yet been
divorced. His wedding was reported racily and with unconscious irony
in the *New York Journal* in May 1855:

LILIAN'S HUB AND BUB
PRETTY POLLY TAKES A NEW HUBBY IN HOBOKEN
WITH SOLOMON IN ALL HIS GLORY SHE RETURNS TO ROCK THE
CRADLE IN NEW YORK

Miss Lilian Russell changed her name to Mrs Edward Solomon yesterday, and the church blessed the union . . . Black was the predominant shade of the bride's outfit, but her cheerful face took off the gloom from her attire.

With his sweetest smile, Mr Solomon was radiant in a buttonhole rose and a fine broadcloth suit, topped with a shiny spring hat. He felt good and he did not care who knew it . . .

(Lilian Russell had only just been divorced from Harry Braham, by whom she had a child.)

. . . Mr and Mrs Solomon returned to their home, and the first thing she did was to kiss her child. Edward looked on beamingly and gave the youngster a fatherly pat.

. . . 'Yes, it's all over', said Mr Solomon, 'and now we hope to lead a quiet home life, away from the public gaze. Our stage existence will always be open to criticism, favourable we hope and trust.

(There was a rumour going round that Solomon had a wife and children in London. When asked about it, Lilian Russell's divorce lawyer told the *Journal* reporter:)

There is nothing in it . . . I know Mr Solomon was never married before. Neither is he the father of a family.

The rumour that Mr Solomon was previously married probably arises from the fact that he was accompanied to this country about two years ago by Miss Edith Blande, who played in Solomon's opera, *The Vicar of Bray*.

Teddy Solomon got away with his 'marriage' to Lilian Russell for a year, then he rashly returned to London and was arrested for bigamy on the petition of his indignant mother-in-law, Clara Isaacs, who had been supporting her daughter Jane and her granddaughter for the past eleven years. However, Solomon's case dragged on for months; the magistrate kept adjourning it because the prosecution failed to produce a witness from America of Solomon's bigamous marriage. In the end Solomon was discharged.

15. Edward Solomon, a brilliant composer who once rivalled Sullivan, wrote *The Nautch Girl* for the Savoy after Gilbert and Sullivan had quarrelled.

Lilian Russell survived the shock and went on to become the leading star of the light musical stage in New York. As for Teddy Solomon, he went bankrupt for £1,000 and paid his creditors a shilling on the pound in 1887. He soon got on his feet again, thanks to generous loans from Arthur Sullivan and other friends.

It never seemed to worry Teddy Solomon if he sold the same song twice, but it got him into embarrassing situations with music publishers and stage producers, and gave him a bad name. A wonderful impromptu pianist, he often obtained a 'deposit' or option from

109

theatre managements for a 'new operetta' which existed only in his imagination. Sidney Grundy, one of his collaborators, once received this telegram from Solomon: 'Come to Cavour next door Alhambra lunch at 1. We play our new opera to Alhambra directors at 3.'

Grundy met him at the old Cavour restaurant, Leicester Square, in a daze because he knew nothing about their new piece. 'Never mind that', said Solomon. 'You tell them a story of Indians – stolen white face – battle – arrival of American rescuers – burning stake – spectacular ballet – and all will be well and the deposit – £200 – will be ours.' It all went like clockwork when Solomon and Grundy met the unmusicianly directors of the Alhambra after lunch. Teddy Solomon improvised brilliantly, 'The Grand March of the Sioux Indians over the Bridge', 'The Love Song of the Pale White-face', 'The Battle of the Forest' and 'The Grand Ballet before the Burning at the Stake'. The directors thought it sounded a great show and gave Solomon £200 for the score which-never-was.

The Nautch Girl by George Dance with music by Solomon opened at the Savoy on June 30, 1891. The *Times* notice began:

'That a slight element of melancholy should mar the festivities attending the production of a new comic opera last night was inevitable. For the first time in the history of the theatre the entertainment was provided with other hands than those of the collaborators for whom it was built ... Mr D'Oyly Carte has done most wisely in going as far as possible on the old lines, and in his choice of a librettist and a composer he has been wonderfully fortunate. Mr George Dance and Mr Edward Solomon have produced a work which ... superficial observers would unhesitatingly class among the Gilbert and Sullivan operas.'

However, it is doubtful if W.S. Gilbert would ever have offered his audience a preposterous plot of this kind. The story centres on a love affair between a Rajah's son and a Nautch girl. When it is revealed late in the piece that she is really a high caste Brahmin, it makes all the difference in the world and instead of him lowering himself to marry her, the tables are turned. *The Nautch Girl* was carried to success by Solomon's lively score and the performances of Rutland Barrington as the Rajah and Jessie Bond as his impoverished relation.

When *The Nautch Girl* came off, Carte presented a revival of

The Vicar of Bray by Solomon and Grundy. The famous Vicar of Bray, who was always ready to bend with the wind of religious change, had nothing to do with this comic opera. Solomon's score had several good numbers in it and Rutland Barrington made a splendid Vicar. But the plot was thin and the humour often rather forced. The vicar and his church people decide to fraternize with the members of a theatrical company and things get a little out of hand. *The Vicar of Bray* didn't interest the public the second time round and departed from the Savoy after a very short stay.

Arthur Sullivan and Sidney Grundy began work on *Haddon Hall,* their new piece, in the autumn. In the meantime Tom Chappell, the music publisher, a personal friend of Sullivan's, had managed to persuade him and Gilbert to bury the hatchet. The latter was far more inclined to do so after the difficulties he had when collaborating with Alfred Cellier. Sullivan wrote to Gilbert on October 4:

Dear Gilbert,

I am quite ready to let bygones be bygones and to meet you at all times in the most friendly spirit, provided that the disagreeable events of the past eighteen months are not alluded to . . .

Gilbert replied the following day in a hopeful strain.

Grim's Dyke – 5 Oct. '91.

. . . It is perhaps unnecessary to assure you that all feeling of bitterness has long since passed from my mind – but there remains a dull leaden feeling that I have been treated with inexplicable unfairness by an old and valued friend with whom I have been en rapport for many years and with whose distinguished name I had had the good fortune to find my own indissolubly linked in a series of works which are known . . . wherever the English tongue is spoken. This is the present state of my mind as regards our relations towards one another, and if you can suggest any reasonable means

111

whereby this cloud can be removed, it will give me infinite pleasure to adopt it.

Yours very truly,

W.S.G.

Sullivan answered promptly:

1 Queens Mansions,
Victoria St.
6th Oct. '91.

Dear Gilbert,

Let us meet and shake hands, and if you still wish to discuss the question of the affidavit (which was also the point upon which I felt most aggrieved) we can do so later. We can dispel the cloud hanging over us by setting up a counter-irritant in the form of a cloud of smoke...

Yours sincerely,

Arthur Sullivan.

This was, of course, a heavy-handed way of suggesting that he and Gilbert should meet and smoke a pipe together.

7 Oct., '91.

Dear Sullivan,

I shall be very pleased to call on you – next Monday at 12 if that will suit you. I hope we may come to an understanding upon the points of difference between us as will render it unnecessary to do as much as allude to them again.

Yours very truly,

W.S.G.

The collaborators had an amicable meeting at Sullivan's flat at Queens Mansions. Gilbert and Sullivan agreed to forget all about the past unpleasantness, shook hands, and became good friends again. Soon afterwards Sullivan left London and settled down at his villa at Roquebrune near Monte Carlo with his nephew, Herbert, and his staff to continue work on *Haddon Hall*.

But his kidney complaint flared up at Roquebrune, causing him more pain than he had ever had before. On New Year's Day, 1892, he had to drag himself to his desk. He managed to carry on working till the end of February, although in great pain. Then he was attacked by shivering fits and forced to go to bed, and had to be given morphia. He went into a coma for a time, but rallied in May, and then had a relapse. The composer was convinced he was dying, and Herbert Sullivan and his valet and housekeeper were seriously alarmed. At Herbert's suggestion they gave him a hot bath and he immediately felt better; it is even possible that the hot bath saved his life. By the end of the month Sullivan had recovered sufficiently to be able to travel back to London.

But the severe illness had slowed up his brain; at first he made little progress on the score of *Haddon Hall* and only gradually regained his facility for composition. This comic opera was loosely based on the story of Dorothy Vernon's elopement from Haddon Hall in order to marry her Catholic lover. Sidney Grundy padded out the slender story by bringing in a Highlander, the Mc'Crankie, who speaks anglicised Scotch and dances his native fling, and some exaggerated Puritan characters with names like Sing-Song Simon and Barnabas Bellow-to-mend. 'The great weakness of the libretto is ... the dramatic insignificance of the main characters who do nothing to make us care for them', said the *Daily Telegraph*.

Lucille Hill had the rather thankless task of playing Dorothy Vernon; other leading parts were played by Rosina Brandram, Courtice Pounds and Rutland Barrington. 'But the music of *Haddon Hall* remains among the best that bears Sir Arthur Sullivan's name' said the *Daily Telegraph*. Sullivan's numbers included a madrigal, 'Now step lightly, hold me tightly', 'The Sun's in the Sky', 'The Earth is Fair' and 'The budding blooms of spring'. *Haddon Hall* ran for 205 performances. While it was still on, Gilbert and Sullivan started work on a new comic opera.

113

In Town was still playing to crowded houses at the Gaiety and there was a happy feeling in the air. George Edwardes happened to travel down on the train to Brighton with Jimmy Davis, an improvident journalist, who annoyed him by saying that *In Town* was a dull show. Davis boasted that he could write something miles better! The Guv'nor bet him he could never do it as he'd never written a piece in his life! However, a few days later Jimmy Davis sent him a most entertaining 'book' entitled *A Gaiety Girl.*

Edwardes accepted it at once and commissioned Sidney Jones, a promising composer who had written numbers for Gaiety burlesques, to write the score. *A Gaiety Girl* had a romantic story about an innocent Gaiety girl who falls in love with a young man of good family. He marries her in the end despite fierce competition from a hard-boiled debutante. It had amusing dialogue, some humorous situations and plenty of scope for George Edwardes to bring on the Gaiety girls in gorgeous clothes. Jimmy Davis, its author, had to use a nom-de-plume and, as he was usually 'owing all' to his creditors, he called himself Owen Hall.

A Gaiety Girl, which opened at the Prince of Wales's on October 14, 1893, had a most tuneful score by Sidney Jones in addition to Owen Hall's witty book. The public flocked to see it, the main attractions being the Gaiety chorus, all hand-picked by the Guv'nor, and beautiful Maud Hobson as Alma Somerset, the heroine. *A Gaiety Girl,* an ideal show for light-hearted audiences, ran for over 400 performances, after being transferred to Daly's Theatre.

Having produced two smash hit musical comedies, George Edwardes decided to concentrate on these pieces in future. In order to plan ahead, he signed up a talented team of composers, librettists and lyric-writers to write musical comedies for the Gaiety. The composers consisted of Ivan Caryll, who also conducted the orchestra at the Gaiety, Sidney Jones and Lionel Monckton; the librettists were James Tanner, author of *In Town,* and Owen Hall; and the principal lyrist was Adrian Ross.

It was a nostalgic occasion at the Savoy on October 7, 1893, when D'Oyly Carte presented *Utopia Ltd.,* the thirteenth Gilbert and

114

Sullivan opera. The piece had altered considerably from Gilbert's original conception; at the last moment he had specially written the leading part of Princess Zara for his protegée, Nancy McIntosh, a beautiful young American singer without any stage experience. Sullivan had been so slowed down by his illness that he only finished his score a week before the first night. With Carte's approval, Gilbert had spent £7,000 on the production of *Utopia Ltd.,* making it the most expensive piece of all; the gorgeous settings included an idyllic South Sea island and a drawing room presentation of debutantes, based on the ceremony at Buckingham Palace. The atmosphere on the first night seemed just like the old days, with the regular patrons keyed up to applaud a piece by their beloved collaborators.

Utopia Ltd. was a satire on almost every aspect of the British way of life; the performance went very well, although Nancy McIntosh, a victim of first night nerves, was a disappointment as Princess Zara. Rutland Barrington as King Paramount, the long-suffering ruler of Utopia, worked with might and main to make a success of the piece, ably assisted by Walter Passmore in the role of Tarantara, the Public Exploder. At the end the audience roared themselves hoarse when Gilbert and Sullivan took their call together and shook hands on the stage.

There were several glowing notices of *Utopia Ltd.* although the *Daily News* commented, 'It was recognized that the first act could be better for being shortened', and the *Pall Mall Gazette* said brutally: 'It is always a melancholy business when a writer is driven to repeat himself. *Utopia Ltd.* is a mirthless travesty of the work with which Gilbert's name is most genuinely associated. The quips, jests, the theory of topsy-turvy, the principle of paradox, the law of the unlikely, seem to have grown old in a single night.'

It was quite true that Gilbert had repeated himself in this piece; he had been making fun of the British and their institutions for so long that he had hardly anything fresh to say. The comic opera took place in the South Sea kingdom of Utopia, which has just decided to adopt a democratic Government. King Paramount has sent his daughter, Princess Zara, to England to be educated at Girton. She returns home with six 'flowers of progress' from England to show

115

King Paramount how to run his country. The best scene in this rather blatant satire was a send-up of the Court of St James, depicted in the style of a Christy minstrel show.

Several of Sullivan's numbers recalled gems from his past scores, but nothing came near 'Take a pair of sparkling eyes' and 'I have a song to sing–O'. *Utopia Ltd.* ran for 245 performances, but it had been such an expensive undertaking that the Savoy lost money on the production. In America *Utopia Ltd.* was a dismal failure. It began to look as if the great collaborators had had their day and would never write another *Mikado* or *Gondoliers*. In any case the public taste had changed, and many people preferred a lighter type of musical play than Gilbert and Sullivan. D'Oyly Carte, a cultured man and a good musician, had far higher standards than his rivals in the field; in a letter to Gilbert, lamenting the fate of *Utopia Ltd.,* he admitted, 'There is no doubt in my mind that what the public want now is simply 'fun' and little else.'

In the autumn of 1894 everyone at the Gaiety was buzzing with excitement as George Edwardes began to rehearse *The Shop Girl*, his most ambitious musical comedy to date. Ivan Caryll had composed the score with additional numbers by Lionel Monckton, and the 'book' was by H.J. Dam. The principals were Ada Reeve, a very vivacious singing star from the music halls, who played the shop girl; Seymour Hicks, an excellent light comedian; and Teddy Payne, a low comedian with a lisp who excelled in song and dance numbers and grotesque impersonations. George Grossmith, Junior, was making his debut at the Gaiety as a masher called Beautiful Bouncing Bertie. Ada Reeve, the shop girl, hadn't told the Guv'nor that she was pregnant; she managed to keep it a secret for the first months of the run, then Ellaline Terriss took over the name part.

When the curtain rose on *The Shop Girl* on November 1, 1894, George Edwardes felt he was on the crest of the wave. The Gaiety was packed to the rafters with an audience which had come to see a colourful show, to admire the Gaiety girls and to laugh at the antics of Teddy Payne as a fantastic shopwalker. The Guv'nor took a last look at the set, then turned his back on the stage in order to watch the public reaction to his new piece.

CHAPTER ELEVEN

THE PEACOCK AND THE GENTLEMAN

At the Gaiety . . . Ivan Caryll found himself at last deservedly playing second fiddle to Lionel Monckton.

GERVASE HUGHES, *COMPOSERS OF OPERETTAS,* 1962

Right from the opening chorus the audience went wild about *The Shop Girl,* a slight story of an attractive girl who serves in a store and charms all the customers and, after a few misunderstandings, agrees to marry her sweetheart, a young medical student. 'The performance was a triumph for all concerned', said the *Times.* And the *Daily Chronicle* declared, 'Mr Edwardes never had a body of vocal comedians more determined to do their best for a novelty.' *The Shop Girl* broke all records for the theatre and ran for 546 performances.

Every night before the performance a fine pair-horse Victoria with a coachman and footman used to drive up to the Gaiety stage door, and a dark, bearded man in evening dress would jump out and hurry inside. This distinguished personage, often mistaken for a Russian nobleman, would walk on to the stage looking like a fashion plate and take a bow. As Ivan Caryll made his way to the orchestra pit the musicians applauded him by tapping on their instruments, having been ordered to do so. Caryll had written the score of *The Shop Girl* and also conducted the Gaiety orchestra.

Felix Tilkins, which was Caryll's real name, had emigrated to England from Belgium in his youth. At first he had known hard times and earned his living by giving music lessons to women in the suburbs; he was so poor that he often had to go without a proper meal. Then he sold some numbers to George Edwardes and was put under contract. Though the public knew him as Ivan Caryll, everybody in the theatre called him Felix. When conducting he used to sit as near the footlights as possible and watch the artistes like a hawk when they were singing. Though not a big man, great force radiated from him;

16. Adrian Ross, the leading lyric writer after W.S. Gilbert, was also a Cambridge scholar. He worked mainly on musical plays for George Edwardes at the Gaiety and Daly's.

when he was conducting his big concerted numbers and finales, he would suddenly swing his body right round and appear to sweep the orchestra along with him during the passage.

Ivan Caryll never looked back after *The Shop Girl*. He composed the scores of nearly all the Gaiety musical comedies for the next decade, in collaboration with Lionel Monckton, and also established himself as the best conductor of light music in England. The Guv' nor had a superstition about keeping a 'girl' in the titles of his shows, so

17. Ivan Caryll, a Belgian composer, wrote musical comedies and operettas and conducted the Gaiety orchestra. He lived like a prince and emigrated to America where he wrote many hit musical plays.

The Shop Girl was followed by *My Girl, The Circus Girl* and *A Runaway Girl*. Whenever Caryll felt in a creative mood, he sat down and composed in a fever of activity until he had completed the work; his scores were noted for big swirling waltzes and semi-operatic finales.

Caryll prided himself on being one of the best dressed men in town; he was most extravagant and spent money as soon as he earned it. This peacock was in his element driving up to the Gaiety in his

Victoria, then hearing the audience's applause as he walked on to the stage and took his bow. He became renowned for his lavish hospitality; he used to entertain his theatrical friends in princely style, was an excellent host and very popular. Geraldine Ulmar, his first wife, has been mentioned as a Gilbert and Sullivan star.

In the new century Caryll wrote the scores of *The Little Cherub, The Earl and the Girl* and *The Duchess of Dantzig,* a comic opera based on the story of Napoleon and Madame Sans Gene, the washerwoman who married Marshal Lefebre and was created a duchess. Produced at the Lyric on October 17, 1903, the *Daily Telegraph* described Ivan Caryll's music as 'well-graced' and said, 'There were some points of vocal excellence.' Caryll was called the ideal composer for this kind of operetta because of 'the Gallic feeling that underlies so much of his music and a ready vein of melody which... has a tenderness and a quite individual charm...' Holbrook Blinn played Napoleon to the Madame Sans Gene of Evie Greene. Though Blinn never had to sing a note, 'he walked away with the laurel wreath for an admirable and clear-cut piece of acting which was the night's most magnetic feature'.

During the run of the piece Caryll took a luxurious suite of rooms at the Carlton Hotel, Haymarket, where he entertained the cast and his many friends every night. There were times when his extravagance landed him in trouble; his creditors would start to press for their accounts and he had a few narrow escapes from the sheriff's officer. An excellent judge of a Continental piece which would adapt into English, he often took trips to Paris and elsewhere in search of new musical plays.

At the Gaiety Ivan Caryll began to get jealous of Lionel Monckton, his collaborator, who invariably wrote the most popular numbers in the shows. Monckton had composed 'A Little Bit of String' for Ellaline Terriss; 'Soldiers in the Park', sung by Grace Palotta, 'Follow the Man from Cook's', and 'Maisie', which Rosie Boote sang in 'The Messenger Boy'.

Lionel Monckton, who came from a legal family, would never have been taken for a musical comedy composer in a month of

18. Lionel Monckton collaborated with Caryll on the first musical comedies and always wrote the most popular numbers. He composed *The Quaker Girl* and several other operettas; he also discovered Gertie Millar and promptly married her.

Sundays. A sombre bachelor, he dressed as if he was on his way to his law chambers, and was as different to Ivan Caryll as chalk to cheese. Tall, broad shouldered, with a deliberate step, he impressed people as a man engaged in weighty matters. Unlike Caryll, he was a meticulous artist who polished his numbers many times before he was satisfied with them. He sometimes wrote his own lyrics under the name of Leslie Mayne, or roughed them out for Adrian Ross to embellish.

His mother, Lady Monckton, a fine amateur pianist, had taught him to play the piano. He showed musical promise at Charterhouse, where he played the organ in the school chapel. He read Law at Oxford, but after joining the dramatic society he started writing songs for their shows and got bitten with the theatre bug. He practised as a barrister for a few years, then threw it up and became a music and drama critic on the *Daily Telegraph,* working under Clement Scott. George Edwardes bought his first songs for the Gaiety, then gave him a contract to write additional numbers for his musical comedies. Unfortunately, Monckton developed rather late as a composer; in his thirties he was still adapting French operettas and writing additional numbers.

Monckton was a great gourmet, liable to upset West End restaurants by sending a dish back to the chef. 'You hardly ever got anything to eat with Lionel', his sister-in-law, Mrs Miskin, once told a friend. His caustic wit made him unpopular at times, but that didn't seem to worry him. He adored cats and dogs, and used to bring his favourite Yorkshire terrier to first nights where it sat obediently under his stall. He was a friend of Arthur Sullivan's and greatly admired his music.

Although George Edwardes knew very little about music, he had a knack of spotting a hit song. Monckton called Edwardes 'Blue-eyed George' because of his way of glancing up at people with his blue eyes, looking as innocent as a new-born babe as he discussed a new contract. Monckton was an eccentric; sometimes he used to stand outside the Gaiety with a checking meter which recorded the number of people who went up in the gallery; later he checked the numbers going into the pit. Nobody ever discovered why he did it – perhaps he wanted to see if the Guv'nor was exagerrating when he declared his latest show was doing wonderful business.

In the nineties a large man in glasses, with a dangerous habit of reading a book and consulting time-tables as he walked about London, often crossed the Strand on his way to the old Gaiety Theatre. Arthur Ropes, who wrote lyrics for George Edwardes under the nom-de-plume of Adrian Ross, looked every inch a scholar, and in fact was a Cambridge Wrangler and a Fellow of King's College. He wrote more lyrics for the Guv'nor's musical plays than anybody else and was probably the best lyrist in England after W.S. Gilbert. The first time Adrian Ross went to a rehearsal at the Gaiety he was so shy that when two chorus girls started to speak to him he took fright and fled to the stage door.

Ross wrote the lyrics of *Joan of Arc,* one of the last Gaiety burlesques, which starred Arthur Roberts, the great gagster, in the role of the Constable of France. Lord Randolph Churchill had just resigned in a huff from the Salisbury Government and gone off to shoot big game in Africa. Roberts walked on to the stage wearing a topee and tropical rig, and carrying a gun, and sang:

> I'm a regular Randy Pandy O
> They call me Jack the Dandy O.

The audience laughed their heads off at Roberts' imitation of the disgrunted politician; but when Lord Randolph returned from safari he went and saw the Gaiety skit, which infuriated him, and persuaded the Censor to cut it out. Adrian Ross was part author of *In Town*, the first musical comedy, which had starred Arthur Roberts. He wrote lyrics for nearly all the Gaiety shows and also contributed lyrics to operettas at Daly's. And in the new century he wrote the lyrics of the English version of *The Merry Widow* when Edwardes presented it at Daly's.

Adrian Ross and Lionel Monckton, who often worked together on musical plays, were close friends outside the theatre. Both of them had a facility for words and took great pleasure in solving acrostics and other kinds of word puzzles. Ross was a very generous man and too kind for his own good; if an actor called on him with a hard luck story, Ross nearly always gave him money. In 1901 he married Ethel Wood, who had acted under the name of Elsie Wilde as it was not considered quite proper to be an actress in the 'nineties. The Guv'nor sent them a fine period clock and a grand piano as a wedding present. Adrian Ross was prematurely white-haired, but his wife, Ethel, looked so young that she sometimes got mistaken for his daughter.

A meticulous writer, Ross polished his verses to the utmost degree. He spoke many languages, including Russian, and had several interests away from the theatre; he wrote a history of Europe and other books on serious subjects. Ethel used to get worried if he got late on his lyrics for George Edwardes, and sometimes tried her hand at roughing out a lyric for him. In the early days of their marriage, when they were rather hard up, Ethel took up journalism and wrote women's articles for the popular press. She became an expert at sending away theatre people who called at the door to ask Ross for a loan that would never be repaid.

Ross was rather a sedentary person and didn't play games, but he could amuse himself for hours playing Patience. He was in the middle of a hand, and had just got out all the queens, when the doctor came in to announce that their first baby was a girl – and that's the reason why she was called Patience! A very religious man, Ross attended his Congregationalist church every Sunday; he was never heard to swear at home, the only words he used being 'Confound it!' The family lived for a long time in Addison Road, Kensington.

His lyrics were of such high quality that he was rarely short of work. But Edwardes, his principal employer, had been paying for his lyrics at a flat rate in the 'nineties. Ethel, realizing he would be far better off if he received royalties on his lyrics, persuaded him to go and see the Guv'nor at the Gaiety. In view of their long association, Edwardes agreed to pay him royalties in future. Adrian Ross came home feeling like the conquering hero, but he had no illusions about the difficulties of being married to a poet. This little effort, written for *Punch,* was really dedicated to Ethel. It began:

> The wife of a poet-biographers show it –
> Has happiness rich and rare,
> In rapturous revel he deigns to dishevel
> Her carefully coiffured hair.
>
> He calls her to listen with glances that glisten
> To songs of his sensitive soul,
> While she is discerning by odours of burning
> That cook with her fancies of shilling romances
> Is finding a heaven with X 37
> And dinner is done to a coal!.

Oh, there's nothing that's dreary or hard
In the life of a wife of the bard,
No maiden should choose to reject or refuse
An offer to marry a son of the muse!

During the run of *The Shop Girl*, George Edwardes had been interviewed by the *Evening News*. Knowing he was an old Savoyard, they asked him why he thought some of the Gilbert and Sullivan operas had failed. Edwardes replied: 'Mr Gilbert used to polish his work to the minutest degree, then he would absolutely refuse to have it altered in any way...I think that sometimes Mr Gilbert would have found it better to alter and experiment. This might have saved a fine work like *Ruddigore*.'

W.S. Gilbert, who had never liked George Edwardes, bitterly resented it when he became the leading impresario of musical plays in the 'nineties. After reading Edwardes's remarks in the paper he replied as follows:

> Mr Edwardes is quite right in supposing that after polishing up my work to the minutest degree, I have not been in the habit of handing it over to the stage manager to embellish with alterations and additions at his pleasure. If I had done so the Savoy pieces would no doubt have borne a stronger resemblance to the productions with which Mr Edwardes's name is associated, but that was not the object I had in view.

Meanwhile D'Oyly Carte was at his wit's end trying to find a piece for the Savoy in 1894. He had been banking on a revival of *The Mikado*, a cast-iron certainty; but Gilbert stated that Nancy McIntosh must play Yum-Yum or he would not give his permission. After her debut in *Utopia Ltd*. Gilbert had adopted her as his daughter, the truth being that he was infatuated with Miss McIntosh and determined to try and make her a star. However, Carte and Sullivan had not been at all impressed with Nancy McIntosh when she played Princess Zara in *Utopia Ltd*. and would not allow her to play Yum-Yum. This infuriated Gilbert, who refused to allow *The Mikado* to be performed at the Savoy, and also banned Carte from producing any other Gilbert and Sullivan operas.

Carte suggested to Sullivan that he might work on a piece for the Savoy with F.C. Burnand, his original collaborator. Burnand envied

Gilbert for having Sullivan to set all his pieces; but he had no new work ready, and therefore re-furbished *La Contrabandista*, the operetta he and Sullivan had written nearly thirty years ago for the German Reeds. Burnand and Sullivan gave the piece a new title, *The Chieftain* but it failed at the Savoy, just as it had done at St George's Hall in the sixties.

W.S. Gilbert joined forces with Dr Osmond Carr, a much younger composer than Sullivan, and produced *His Excellency* at the Lyric on October 27, 1894. The moral of this piece about a Governor who is an inveterate practical joker, is that if you keep playing practical jokes you will end up by being degraded to the ranks. The *Daily Telegraph* called the 'book', 'one of the best that has come from the most ingenious and successful of modern librettists'. Once more Gilbert scourged the follies of the day, but inevitably the piece suffered from its score and the general opinion was that if Sullivan had written it, *His Excellency* would have run a year. 'Dr Osmond Carr sometimes droops in his flight through a long evening ... sometimes lapses into the commonplace ... and his music is understandably imitative of Sullivan', said one critic, George Grossmith, Rutland Barrington, Jessie Bond and Alice Barnett all gave admirable performances, while Nancy McIntosh played a secondary role. But in spite of all the talents employed in *His Excellency,* it only ran for 161 performances.

George Edwardes planned to produce light operettas in addition to his musical comedies at the Gaiety, and in 1895 he took over Daly's Theatre for this purpose. His first piece to have its premiere there, *An Artist's Model,* was by Owen Hall and Sidney Jones. Daly's, a most elegant playhouse, had been built in the Florentine style of the Italian Renaissance and its auditorium was constructed on the cantilver principle. The decor was a mixture of red, gold, silver and bronze, the front of the dress circle and the boxes were adorned with boat-loads of sea-nymphs and Cupids blowing bubbles.

Before the Guv'nor put *An Artist's Model* into rehearsal, he cabled Marie Tempest, who had gone to act in America soon after her triumph in *Dorothy,* offering her a big contract to come back to

England to be leading lady at Daly's. Marie Tempest accepted his proposition at once and sailed home on the first boat.

The Guv'nor greeted her in his luxurious office at Lisle Street at the back of Daly's, mesmerising her with his charm and enthusiasm to such an extent that she hardly took a second look at her contract. Then he handed her the libretto of *An Artist's Model*; but when she read it she nearly had a fit. There was a marvellous part in it for Letty Lind as a teenage heiress on her own in Paris – but no part at all for her! George Edwardes blandly admitted that he had forgotten to ask Owen Hall to write in her part. But Marie Tempest had lost her temper and started to walk out of the office. 'Now, my dear, don't worry', said Edwardes soothingly. 'You just go away for a little holiday, and when you come back I promise you it will be written in for you!'

Won over by his blarney, Marie Tempest agreed to go and take a holiday. When she returned she found her part, her music and her lyrics all ready for her and went straight into rehearsals of *An Artist's Model*. Edwardes had engaged Hayden Coffin to play opposite Marie Tempest, thus re-uniting the two stars of *Dorothy*. The principal comedian was Huntley Wright, and the other leading part was played by Letty Lind, a pretty blonde with a pleasing voice who was an extremely graceful dancer. Marie Tempest made a contrast to Letty Lind: petite and brunette, she was a superb singer and a first rate comedienne with a magnetic personality. In the new century she became one of the most dazzling stars of the British stage and had her name in electric lights when she was well over sixty.

CHAPTER TWELVE

THE ORPHEUS OF DALY'S

Round the turn of the century Sidney Jones alone played as positive a role in operettas as that other Jones who preferred to be known as Edward German.

GERVASE HUGHES, *COMPOSERS OF OPERETTAS*, 1962

An Artist's Model, which George Edwardes presented at Daly's on February 2, 1895, had several delightful numbers in the score by Sidney Jones, but Owen Hall's 'book' was uneven and a trifle vulgar in places. As the Guv'nor watched the first night audience, he knew the piece was dragging and sensed that the house was growing restless. After the curtain fell a few young men in the pit started to boo. The Guv'nor walked on to the stage as cool as a cucumber and asked the audience what they thought of *An Artist's Model.* 'Half and half!' shouted the gallery. 'Well, come back in five or six weeks and I'll have the other half put right', retorted the Guv'nor.

The *Daily Telegraph* said, 'Mr Owen Hall, having to hand two performers exceptionally well versed in the ways of romance upon the lighter lyric boards (Marie Tempest and Hayden Coffin) takes as his mainstay the story of the two lovers.' Hayden Coffin was Rudolph, a painter in Paris who still pines for his old love, Adele (Marie Tempest) who left him and married a millionaire. She returns to Paris a widow, but engaged now to a British peer. In Act two all the main characters turn up at a ball at a stately home, and Adele discovers, just in the nick of time, that she doesn't really love her peer and goes back to Rudolph.

The *Daily Telegraph* continued: 'Much of Mr Sidney Jones's music has set our heads nodding and appealed even more deeply to

19. Exterior, Daly's Theatre, Leicester Square with five favourite actresses super- ▷ imposed: (l to r) Adrienne Augarde, Pauline Chase, Madge Lessing, Billie Burke and Gabrielle Ray.

the ears of musicians. Mr Harry Greenbank furnishes ... stanzas that lack neither point nor polish. Mr Sidney Jones's ballads have an agreeable, melodic flow, and lie gracefully for the voice; his sprightly pieces are no less engaging while his orchestration shows an experienced and refined touch.'

Letty Lind, as an adventurous heiress, brought the house down with her ditty about a wren and a fascinating tom tit. 'Her singing of the mock-pathetic lay was followed by a dance which, with the quaint little hop and flutter, was a thing to be seen ... with all the impudence of a small bird she cocked her head, flapped her arms and swung her scintillating skirt hither and thither ... Both as a vocalist and as an

actress, Miss Marie Tempest has gained strength and her performance of a superlatively difficult part set her once more on the pinnacle of popularity.'

The Farewell Waltz, a duet sung by Marie Tempest and Hayden Coffin in the ballroom, was probably the best number. Harry Greenbank also wrote a witty lyric poking fun at the 'new art' of the period:

> Though pictures as a connoisseur I don't pretend to criticise,
> I know the points in painting that will make for notoriety –
> A limb that's rather shapely, or a hand and foot of pretty size,
> With just a slight suspicion of a proper impropriety.
> The age that reads the Yellow Book delights to find how blue it is.
> Today's artistic idols are to-morrow's on-the-shelfy ones;
> But I prefer to Beardsley and his female incongruities
> The highly coloured posters that are genuine Adelphi ones.

George Edwardes, having decided *An Artist's Model* needed drastic cutting and re-writing, called in Owen Hall and Sidney Jones and also James Tanner, the Gaiety librettist. They joined forces and reconstructed the piece from start to finish, and did their work so well that *An Artist's Model* ran for 405 performances at Daly's.

Sidney Jones, who composed the first four operettas at Daly's for George Edwardes, was the son of an Army bandmaster. Sidney Jones used to play the clarinet as a little boy in his father's band, dressed in a miniature uniform. He became a bandmaster, like his father, then branched out as a theatre conductor, and went on tours with operas in the provinces and in Australia. Later, he wrote *Linger Longer Lou,* which Ellaline Terriss sang at the Gaiety. Then George Edwardes put him under contract as a composer and later appointed him conductor of Daly's orchestra.

Of medium height, Jones had a small, neat moustache and looked rather like a business man. While conducting at a Leeds theatre he fell in love with Hannah Mary Linley, a good looking chorus girl, and soon married her. While they were courting, the 'boys' in the band

20. Sidney Jones composed the first four operettas at Daly's in the 'nineties, including *The Geisha,* which co-starred Marie Tempest and Hayden Coffin.

used to chaff him for gazing up at his beloved on the stage and sometimes missing a bar of the music. Sidney Jones put his heart into his music, but was a very good husband who never looked at another woman despite the temptations. After writing a new number, he used to play it over to his wife, Mary, to hear her opinion of it. If he ever thought of a promising theme, he used to make a note on his shirt-cuff or, if he was at home, he made a note on a table-cloth. He seldom went out and about in London and came straight home from Daly's.

The musicians in the forty-piece orchestra at the theatre thought the world of Sidney Jones, a genial conductor who never lost his temper with anybody. On the first anniversary of *A Gaiety Girl,* his musical comedy which had been transferred to Daly's, the orchestra presented him with a charming testimonial; at the top left hand corner was a picture of Maud Hobson, the leading lady, and the wording was as follows:

To Mr Sidney Jones

Daly's Theatre,
London W.

Dear Sir,

We the Members of your Orchestra on the occasion of the anniversary performance of *A Gaiety Girl* desire to offer you (the highly esteemed Composer) our heartiest congratulations upon the phenomenal success of your first Musical Comedy.

With *An Artist's Model* at Daly's and *The Shop Girl* at the Gaiety both doing capacity business, George Edwardes had demonstrated that he could run two theatres successfully with musical plays. It was a different story for Richard D'Oyly Carte, still struggling to find a single winner at the Savoy. It seemed obvious that Gilbert and Sullivan were more successful together than when each of them worked with a different partner. *The Chieftain* by Sullivan and Burnand had failed dismally, and *His Excellency,* Gilbert's clever piece with music by Osmond Carr, had only had a short run. Carte made diplomatic approaches to his friend, Arthur Sullivan, and to W.S. Gilbert and managed to persuade them to forget their last contretemps over Nancy McIntosh being turned down in *The Mikado.* Sullivan, after reading Gilbert's first outline of his new piece, *The Grand Duke,* in August 1895, wrote him the following enthusiastic letter:

River House,
Walton-on-Thames
11 Aug. 1895

My dear Gilbert,

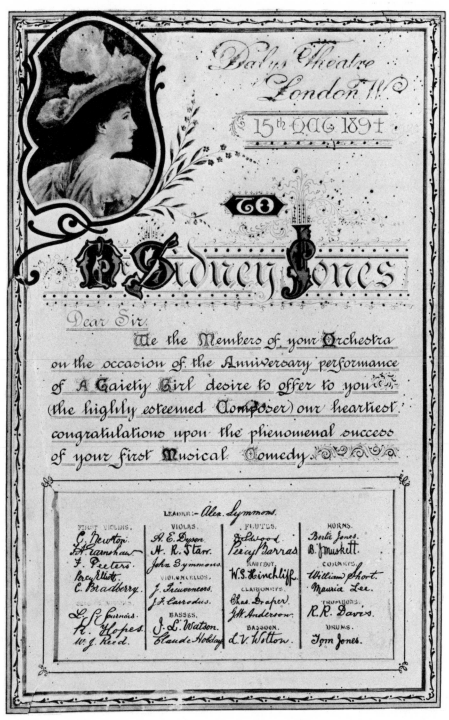

Daly's Theatre
London W.
15th OCT 1894

To

Mr Sidney Jones

Dear Sir,

We the Members of your Orchestra
on the occasion of the Anniversary performance
of A Gaiety Girl desire to offer to you
(the highly esteemed Composer) our heartiest
congratulations upon the phenomenal success
of your first Musical Comedy.

LEADER:- Alex. Symmons.

FIRST VIOLINS.	VIOLAS.	FLUTES.	HORNS.
L. Newton.	A. E. Dyson.	D. Elwood	Bertie Jones.
J. H. Earnshaw.	H. R. Starr.	Percy Barras	B. J. Muskett.
F. Peeters.	John Symmons.	HAUTBOY.	CORNETS.
Percy Elliot.	VIOLONCELLOS.	W. S. Hinchliff.	William Short.
C. Bradberry.	J. Treuveneers.	CLARIONETS.	Maurice Lee.
SECOND VIOLINS.	J. F. Carrodus.	Chas. Draper.	TROMBONE.
L. P. Fournois.	BASSES.	J. H. Anderson.	R. R. Davis.
R. Hopes.	J. L. Watson.	BASSOON.	DRUMS.
W. J. Reed.	Claude Hobday	L. V. Wotton.	Tom Jones.

21. This touching tribute to Sidney Jones from the members of the orchestra at
Daly's was presented to him on the first anniversary of his musical comedy, *A
Gaiety Girl,* on October 15, 1894.

I have studied the sketch plot very carefully, and like it even more than I did when I first heard it on Thursday. It comes out as clear and bright as possible.

I shall be very pleased to set it, and am prepared to begin (as soon as you have anything ready for me) and have written to Carte to tell him so...

Sullivan met Gilbert and D'Oyly Carte at the latter's flat at Adelphi Terrace. Gilbert, in a conciliatory mood, assured them that he had no intention of putting Nancy McIntosh into the new piece, and he agreed to lift the ban on the revival of any comic operas he had written. This enabled Carte to revive several Gilbert and Sullivan operas while the collaborators were in the course of writing *The Grand Duke*.

Gilbert had based his piece on *The Duke's Dilemma*, a short story in *Blackwood's Magazine*. A penniless Grand Duke of a small German state learns that his fiancée, the Princess of Monte Carlo, and her parents are coming on a visit to his Court, which of course is non-existent; so he tries to keep up appearances by hiring a troupe of actors to impersonate his courtiers. *The Grand Duke* started out as a satire on the pretensions of petty royalty in German courts, and on gambling and capital punishment. But as Gilbert developed his plot the satire got watered down; then George Grossmith gave up his part as the Grand Duke and Jessie Bond, another principal, left the company to get married. Eventually Gilbert built *The Grand Duke* round Julia Jellicoe, an English lady whose German is much more fluent than her English – a dig at Queen Victoria. Ilka von Palmay, a clever Hungarian actress, played Julia Jellicoe, but this character held up the action in several places. There were difficulties during rehearsals; Gilbert was hampered by his gout, and Sullivan was in such pain that he had to take injections of morphia.

The Grand Duke was presented at the Savoy on March 7, 1896; Walter Passmore played the Duke and Rutland Barrington was Ludwig, leader of the actors who were posing as courtiers. The piece was well received and had several good notices, but the *Times* led the chorus of disapproval: 'Signs are not wanting that the rich vein which the collaborators and their followers have worked for many years is at last dangerously near extinction.'

Ilka von Palmay and Rutland Barrington made individual successes, but the public showed hardly any interest in *The Grand Duke,* which came off after 126 performances, the shortest run of all the Savoy operas. Gilbert and Sullivan both confided to intimate friends that the other man was to blame for the failure. Gilbert's letter to Mrs Bram Stoker shows he was aware of having written a feeble piece: '. . . now that the baby is born I shall soon recover . . . I'm not at all a proud Mother, and I never want to see the ugly, misshapen little brat again.' D'Oyly Carte recouped the losses on *The Grand Duke* by putting on an extremely popular season of Gilbert and Sullivan revivals.

George Edwardes presented *The Geisha,* a Japanese operetta by Sidney Jones and Owen Hall, at Daly's on April 28, 1896. Its stars were again Marie Tempest and Hayden Coffin; she played the devastating Geisha, O Mimosa San, who flirts harmlessly with Lieutenant Fairfax of the Royal Navy (Hayden Coffin). Molly, his fiancée, (Letty Lind) turns up in Japan and disguises herself as a Geisha to keep an eye on him. But things go wrong when the wicked Marquis Imari decrees he will marry Mimosa San, who loathes him. Wun-Hi, proprietor of the Geisha tea-house, is turned out for defying Imari; Mimosa is rescued by an English visitor from the clutches of Imari; but Molly – still disguised as a Geisha – is picked to replace Mimosa San as Imari's bride. Thanks to the ingenious Mimosa San's impersonation of a fortune teller, Molly escapes and all ends happily.

Edwardes, remembering how Gilbert had insisted on the accuracy of everything Japanese in *The Mikado,* engaged Arthur Dóisy of the Japanese Legation to ensure that the settings and costumes in the piece were authentic. Sidney Jones wrote his finest score for *The Geisha,* which was compared favourably with Sullivan's best work. If Owen Hall's libretto had not been so very far removed from reality, this operetta might have survived as well as the Gilbert and Sullivan operas.

Clement Scott said in *The Illustrated London News*: 'London in

22. Marie Tempest was praised to the skies for her performance as O Mimosa San in *The Geisha*, produced at Daly's in 1896.

23. Letty Lind as Molly Seamore, the delightfully innocent heroine of *The Geisha*. She made a great hit with her singing of 'The Interfering Parrot'.

24. Huntley Wright as Wun-Hi, the comic proprietor of a Geisha tea-house in *The Geisha*. Marie Tempest objected to the way he gagged in the Daly's operettas and ruined some of her numbers.

recent years has seen no more delightful entertainment than the Japanese *Geisha* at Daly's ... Mr Owen Hall's piece is a feast to the eye in colour and a delight to the ear owing to the charming music of Mr Sidney Jones and Mr Lionel Monckton' (who wrote additional numbers).

The *Daily Mail* raved about Letty Lind's performance 'always smiling, singing, romping, captivating all hearts by that indefinable "je ne sais quoi" which Nellie Farren of old used to exercise over the gallery boys ... Miss Marie Tempest achieved another triumph by her dainty beauty and superb singing'.

Huntley Wright as Wun-Hi, the proprietor of the Geisha teahouse who gets evicted by the wicked Marquis Imari, sang 'Chin Chin Chinaman', which got whistled all over the town:

Chin Chin Chinaman
Mucheee mucheee sad!
He afraid Allo trade
Well-ee well-ee bad!
No-ee joke Brokee-broke
Makee shutee shop!
Chin chin Chinaman
Chop, chop, chop!

Marie Tempest scored with her charming number, 'The Amorous Goldfish'. But her rival, Letty Lind, sang 'The Interfering Parrot', one of the best lyrics Harry Greenbank ever wrote:

A parrot once resided in a pretty gilded cage,
Sarcastic was his temper and uncertain was his age.
He knew that two canaries had apartments overhead
Who'd only very recently been wed!
He kept his eye on all that they were doing
An interfering parrot in a nasty frame of mind!
And vowed he'd stop their billing and their cooing
Which really was exceedingly unkind!

Polly winked an eye and Polly gave a sigh
And Polly took his best hat down;

139

He called on Mrs C and took a cup of tea,
When Mr C had gone to town;
Then wisely wagged his head
And seriously said –
'Well, husbands *are* a lot!
A pretty one you've got!
Such tales I never heard!
So dissolute a bird
I never met before!
What goings on! Oh lor!'

Hayden Coffin made a big hit with 'Jack's the Boy', a song about sailors' escapades when they are in port, and Letty Lind had another very popular number, "The Toy Monkey". *The Geisha* ran for 760 performances at the same time as *The Circus Girl* was a big winner at the Gaiety. George Edwardes made a fortune from these pieces, and bought a mansion at Winkfield near Ascot and began to take a great interest in horseracing, investing in a string of top class racehorses and starting his own training establishment at Ogbourne Maisey near Marlborough.

Harry Greenbank, who had written *The Geisha* lyrics, was an extremely modest man and had a retiring disposition and avoided public appearances at first nights if possible. This may have been due to the fact that he had suffered from consumption since he was a boy. Amongst his circle of friends Greenbank was very popular on account of his amiability and his generous nature. It is sad to relate that his career was cut short when he was only 33; in 1898 he had moved out of London and gone to live at Boscombe, Bournemouth, hoping that the milder climate and cleaner atmosphere would benefit his health. But while he was working on the lyrics of *San Toy* for Daly's, he had a relapse.

When George Edwardes heard about it, he sent Harry Greenbank to Davos at his own expense to try and get him cured. And, with typical generosity, he paid Mrs Greenbank a handsome retainer while her husband was away in Switzerland. But the doctors at Davos could do nothing for Greenbank because he had put himself in their hands when it was too late. He returned to England knowing he was a doomed man; at the end of the year his strength ebbed away and he died from a heart attack on February 26, 1899.

Harry Greenbank had few equals as a lyric writer; his work had a brilliancy, spontaneity and a rhythmical smoothness. William Archer had written in his review of *The Geisha*: 'Mr Harry Greenbank has this time surpassed not only himself but all his competitors in the facility and finish of his rhyming . . . Mr Gilbert . . . is the master in this style of work. But more than one of his lyrics Mr Gilbert might sign without a blush.'

The Geisha was a money-spinner all over the English speaking world and repeated its success in Germany and on the Continent. Marie Tempest grew very bossy in the theatre and put on such grand airs that everyone at Daly's called her Maria. She thought that being the leading lady entitled her to order her carriage to wait outside the royal entrance. The genial Guv'nor found her arrogance hard to bear; he called her 'a naughty girl' when they had a row, but avoided a showdown with her, appreciating that Maria with all her faults was the cleverest actress he had ever managed.

When *The Geisha* came off George Edwardes presented *A Greek Slave*, another operetta by Sidney Jones and Owen Hall, on June 8, 1898, with Marie Tempest and Hayden Coffin in the leading roles. The *Daily Telegraph*, amongst others, gave it a rave notice; this operetta was hailed as being on a higher plane than the first two Daly's pieces – 'The book is dramatically and charmingly arranged by Owen Hall and the production is as beautiful as anything that has been seen on the English stage . . . Mr George Edwardes is advancing step by step to the dignity of grand opera . . . but he has not neglected fun, and there is a gloriously decorated stage never innocent of dance and merry jest . . . Apart from the cleverness of the book, the grace of the lyrics and the rare beauty, freshness and attractiveness of the music, the great honours were divided between Mr Hayden Coffin as Diomed, the handsome slave, and Miss Marie Tempest, who, as actress and singer alike, surpassed all she has ever done . . . but it was not only in her great gift of singing, her rare art of expression, and her dramatic delivery that Miss Tempest once again excelled . . . Miss

Marie Tempest holds the stage. Although small of stature, she seems to grow and become taller with the impulse and passion of the moment. Only a rare artist can do that.' In fact, the comedy of Letty Lind as another Greek slave and Huntley Wright as a wizard was eclipsed by the love story of Marie Tempest and Hayden Coffin. The outstanding numbers were 'I want to be popular', 'The golden isle', sung by Marie Tempest, 'The girl of my heart' sung by Hayden Coffin and their duet, 'Forgive'.

Gilbert and Sullivan, after the debacle of *The Grand Duke,* never wrote another comic opera together. D'Oyly Carte commissioned Sullivan to write the score of *The Beauty Stone* from a libretto by A. Conan Doyle and J. Comyns Carr. The latter went to stay with Sullivan at Beaulieu while they were working on the piece and was shocked to see how the composer's appearance had deteriorated. His poor state of health had changed his personality; instead of the good natured man Comyns Carr had known, he was greeted by a petulant semi-invalid. Sullivan took a feverish pleasure in visiting the casino at Monte Carlo every day, sometimes losing a great deal at the tables. He had once said to George R. Sims, 'The bandits have had seven hundred of the best out of me this evening, I've lost every note I brought with me.' 'Never mind', said Sims, 'there are plenty more where they came from.'

 The Beauty Stone had a melodramatic and badly constructed 'book' which gave Sullivan's music little chance to shine. It opened at the Savoy on May 28, 1898, and was a total failure. By an oversight Gilbert never received his tickets for the first night; although Carte and Sullivan apologized to him, Gilbert remained convinced that they had slighted him on purpose. Carte revived *The Sorcerer* to follow *The Beauty Stone.* At the end the audience shouted for Gilbert and Sullivan to take their call, but when the two of them appeared on the stage, Gilbert refused to speak to Sullivan. His boorish behaviour upset Arthur Sullivan very much; nobody could have guessed that this was the last occasion on which the collaborators ever met.

 In November Sullivan was introduced to Captain Basil Hood, an able musical comedy author, by his secretary, Wilfred Bendall.

Sullivan's diary records: 'Hood came; talked over the possibility of doing piece together. I know of no one so good now (putting Gilbert out of the question, of course).' Arthur Sullivan took an instant liking to Basil Hood and agreed to collaborate with him on a comic opera with an eastern setting. He said later: 'Hood is such a nice fellow and so pleasant to work with.'

Sullivan went to Lucerne to write the score of the eastern piece and Hood joined him there. Sullivan was in constant pain; Herbert Sullivan and his faithful staff knew the composer was in failing health, but it was useless to try and stop him working. He returned to England and managed to complete the score of *The Rose of Persia* on November 18. Sullivan was in such pain at the dress rehearsal that he thought the piece was as dull as ditchwater and bound to be a failure. But on the first night at the Savoy on November 29 it was extremely well received.

Basil Hood's book was far more ingenious and witty than the average one for a comic opera. Sullivan's music, more complex than usual, 'was enough to delight the expert and to please the less sophisticated listener... the musician is once again absolutely himself... the composer's rare feeling for the sweet, the beautiful, the humorous and the characteristic in music is still with him,' said the *Daily Telegraph*.

Abu-el Hassan, an eccentric Persain merchant, has a strange habit of giving the beggars of the city hospitality in his house every night. One night the Sultana goes there disguised as a dancing girl. The Sultan hears of the affair and it looks as if Hassan and the Sultana are in danger of losing their heads over it. Hassan takes a drug to banish his fears, and suddenly imagines *he* is the Sultan. Next night the real Sultan visits Hassan's house in disguise, and is amused by Hassan's pretensions and lets him believe he is the Sultan after all. It ends with a slave girl rescuing Hassan and the Sultana from the threat to their lives. Walter Passmore stood out from the others in the role of Hassan – 'his portrait is as whimsical and entertaining as anything he has yet done'. The piece achieved a moderate run of over 200 performances.

The first night of *San Toy* took place at Daly's on October 21, 1899, during a pea-souper, and half the theatre was empty when the curtain rose; but George Edwardes never doubted its success. Sidney Jones had again written the score, but the 'book' was by Edward Morton. Marie Tempest again starred in it with Hayden Coffin, but it was to be her last appearance for the Guv'nor. Her domineering ways had upset the company: she was trying to produce the show at times and the Guv'nor found it increasingly hard to put up with her tantrums. The climax came at the dress rehearsal when Marie Tempest, who hated the long Chinese trousers she had to wear in the role of San Toy, cut them down to shorts, making her look slightly improper. George Edwardes lost his temper and told her that unless she wore the correct Chinese trousers on the first night she must leave Daly's! He was only bluffing, but she replied calmly: 'All right, I'll go!'

Marie Tempest was proud of her singing voice, and hated the comedians at Daly's like Huntley Wright for gagging away on the stage and ruining her numbers. She appeared in *San Toy* as the daughter of a Chinese mandarin (Rutland Barrington) who has to disguise herself as a boy to escape being called up into the Emperor's corps of women soldiers. The rest of the plot mainly concerns her love affair with a British Army officer; one hardly needs to say that he was played by Hayden Coffin. The comedy was in the experienced hands of Huntley Wright and Rutland Barrington.

Mr George Edwardes has triumphed at Daly's by giving the people what they want, said the *Era*. 'This may briefly be described as a succession of amusing and exhilarating songs, rendered with admirable art by ... popular performers; plenty of jokes, and a dazzlingly brilliant spectacle. Mr Edward Morton has written a most promising and ingeniously constructed first act ... The musical numbers are right up to the standard by which we are accustomed to measure the efforts of expert verse writers like the late Mr Harry Greenbank and Mr Adrian Ross and clever composers like Mr Sidney Jones and Mr Lionel Monckton.

Mr Rutland Barrington has never seemed more demurely and artistically droll than as the Mandarin ... The way in which he managed his voice in the song about his 'six little wives' was marvellous ... Mr Hayden Coffin as Captain Bobby Preston was in excellent form both vocally and otherwise. Miss Marie Tempest's cultured vocalism and bright amusing style carried the house with her from her first entrance as San Toy, and she completely fulfilled the expectations of her legions of admirers.'

One of the most popular songs in the piece was 'Rhoda and her Pagoda', an additional number by Lionel Monckton.

Rhoda Rye was an English maid,
Clever and smart was Rhoda,
She served up tea to the highest grade
In a charming Bond Street Pagoda.
And gentlemen thought they gazed upon
An angel imported from Canton,
So perfect her dress – so true the plan
Of the pretty Pagoda that Rhoda ran!

Rhoda, Rhoda ran a Pagoda,
Selling tea and ices and soda,
Many a maiden's hope began
In the pretty Pagoda Rhoda ran.

After *San Toy* had been running for six months Marie Tempest left the cast, and the Guv'nor decided to give her role to Florence Collingbourne, her understudy, who made a tremendous success in it. But Florence Collingbourne suddenly informed him she was getting married and leaving Daly's. The Guv'nor decided to give the part to Ada Reeve, taking a chance that her voice would be strong enough, and she rose to the occasion. *San Toy* went on to run for 768 performances.

Sidney Jones had fallen out with George Edwardes because he preferred to write the complete score of a piece, instead of having numbers by Lionel Monckton and other composers interpolated into it. After *San Toy* he made up his mind to work for other managements who would let him write his own scores, but later he was to regret this decision.

D'Oyly Carte encouraged Arthur Sullivan and Basil Hood to write another comic opera together after *The Rose of Persia*. The composer, then in his late fifties, didn't realize how ill he was and thought he had many years of work ahead of him. Basil Hood went to stay with Sullivan in Monte Carlo in June, 1900, bringing with him an outline of the new piece, *The Emerald Isle*, and some rough lyrics. But Sullivan was composing the music so slowly that Hood thought it would never be finished by the end of the year.

In August Sullivan moved on to Switzerland, hoping to find inspiration in another country. But he caught a cold and even found it a struggle to travel home to London. On his arrival he was asked to compose a Te Deum to celebrate the later successes of the British Army in the South African War. In September he returned to the score of *The Emerald Isle,* working at Shepperton in fits and starts. He wrote a pathetic letter to Helen D'Oyly Carte, who was in charge at the Savoy as her husband was very ill with a digestive ailment and no longer capable of carrying on as manager. D'Oyly Carte had been in poor health for the past three years and used to jump at any opportunity to leave London and spend some time at his house on the Thames at Eyot Island near Shepperton Lock. Sullivan's letter to Helen D'Oyly Carte was as follows:

October 1900

Dear Helen,

> I work hard and waste no time knowingly and wilfully, but I am *very slow* at it. I am so weak I cannot get my strength back and the chill I got in Switzerland has pulled me down dreadfully – my voice is still 'absent without leave' and is the result of general debility...

Sullivan moved on to Tunbridge Wells spa, hoping to find a cure. But his kidney trouble grew worse and left him very weak; a doctor had to give him drugs to ease the pain. When he returned to London he had only written two numbers of *The Emerald Isle,* and done sketches for fifteen others. He visited his mother's grave at Brompton Cemetery on November 2nd, the anniversary of her death, and caught a cold.

On October 21 Sir Arthur Sullivan could only talk in a whisper. Herbert Sullivan, in great alarm, telephoned his doctor, Sir Thomas Barlow, who promised to come and see him the following morning. Herbert Sullivan also notified Mrs Fanny Ronalds of his uncle's grave condition. In the evening Sullivan felt drowsy and went off to sleep. At 6:00 next morning Herbert and the staff were awakened by Sullivan's bell ringing violently. When Herbert rushed into his bedroom with Clothilde Raquet, his housekeeper, and Louis Jager, his valet, the composer was dying. 'My heart! my heart!' he called out and died in Herbert Sullivan's arms.

By the time Sir Thomas Barlow arrrived at Queens Mansions, Arthur Sullivan was dead; Fanny Ronalds also got there too late. He had asked to be buried with all his family in Brompton Cemetery, but at Queen Victoria's recommendation the Dean and Chapter of St Paul's asked that Sullivan should be buried in the crypt of St Paul's Cathedral.

The public were shocked at the unexpected death of their favourite composer; hundreds of people lined the streets to watch the funeral cortege set out for St Paul's. As the cortege procession passed Adelphi Terrace in the Strand, some instinct prompted Richard D'Oyly Carte to get up from his sick bed and go to the window. When told who was on his way to be buried, Carte said, 'I have seen the last of my old friend Sullivan.'

Arthur Sullivan had left more than half the score of *The Emerald Isle* unfinished. The D'Oyly Cartes were in a frantic state, looking for a composer capable of completing the score. Carte knew that Sullivan had a very high opinion of Edward German, a serious composer who had written some first class incidental music for a number of Shakesperian plays. 'There is only one man of genius to follow me, and that is Edward German', he had told Comyns Carr. Before taking a final decision, Carte consulted William Boosey of Chappells. That shrewd judge of musical talent clinched the matter by saying, 'You must ask Edward German if he will complete the score.'

PART 4
Sullivan's Mantle

25. Sir Edward German was regarded as Sullivan's natural successor. Though he composed *Merrie England* and *Tom Jones,* he lacked Sullivan's genius for comic opera, and never fulfilled his promise.

CHAPTER THIRTEEN

THE HERMIT OF MAIDA VALE

Mr German shows so exquisite a sense of the lighter musical forms and is so accomplished a master of the orchestra that Sullivan's place seems to be vacant no longer.

PALL MALL GAZETTE, APRIL 1902

Edward German agreed to undertake the completion of the score of *The Emerald Isle*; he had the greatest admiration for Sir Arthur Sullivan as a composer – and was grateful to him for encouraging his early compositions – and regarded the work as a sacred trust. However, he didn't realize what a formidable task he would have to get the piece ready for production in the following spring. Sullivan had only left a melodic outline of fifteen of the numbers, written in his peculiar musical shorthand. German had to decipher every one of these hieroglyphics before he could write the melodies and orchestrate them. After that, he had to compose eleven brand new numbers in the same style. An extremely conscientious musician, he worked day and night on the score, although he nearly went mad at times trying to decipher Sullivan's musical shorthand. He spent the winter writing the score of *The Emerald Isle* at his home at Hall Road, Maida Vale. Basil Hood visited him often and did his best to clear up any points about the libretto; he had great charm and got along just as well with German as he had done with Sir Arthur Sullivan. They managed to finish *The Emerald Isle* by spring, 1901, as promised.

Richard D'Oyly Carte never recovered from his digestive ailment and died in March 1901; Helen D'Oyly Carte therefore presented *The Emerald Isle* at the Savoy on April 27. It was very well received, though some critics were uncomplimentary about Hood's libretto, saying that it sounded as if Gilbert had written it on an off day. Pat Murphy, a young fiddler who has won the love of Molly O'Grady by pretending to be blind, goes to the caves of Carric-Cleena with the object of faking a cure for his 'blindness' from the little

151

people inside. Terence O'Brian, an Irish patriot, is hiding from the English soldiers in the caves, but the locals save him by frightening the British soldiers away with tales of the little monsters who haunt the caves. Then Professor Bunn, an itinerant conjuror, gives a hair-raising account of how the pixies imprisoned him in the caves. Professor Bunn dominates the rest of the play and restores O'Brian's reputation so that he is free to marry Lady Rosie Pippin, the Lord Lieutenant's daughter.

Walter Passmore as Professor Bunn 'covered himself with glory and sailed through his part with marvellous activity', said the *Daily Telegraph*. His song, 'Imitations', was the hit of the evening. 'His little tricks of legerdemain and droll burlesque of hypnotism' were greatly appreciated by the audience. Robert Evett as Terence O'Brian gave an admirable performance and sang 'I'm descended from Brian Boru' and 'Oh, have you met a man in debt?'. Isabel Jay won all hearts as Lady Rosie Pippin ...' in addition she warbled divinely and acted exquisitely'. 'Only those who know intimately Sullivan's harmonic and instrumental methods will estimate at its true value Mr German's supplementary work ... we have harmony and orchestration designed in the true spirit of the master ...'

The Emerald Isle ran for over 200 performances. Edward German was showered with praise for his vital contribution to the score; in fact the critics overdid it and called him a second Sullivan, which was absurd. How could German possibly compete with Sullivan in the first piece he had ever written for the stage? His melodies were too reminiscent to sound original and, above all, he lacked the wonderful sense of humour that Arthur Sullivan had expressed in his music.

Edward German Jones, as he was christened, had been born on February 17, 1862, at Whitchurch, Shropshire, where he spent his early years. His love of the English countryside and English customs were major influences on his music. His friend Herbert Scott, who grew up with him, wrote in his biography of German that 'as a boy he knew the song of every bird; the trees had tongues for him, so had the fields and flowers, and the rushing brooks were open books ...'

His father, a chemist, was honorary organist at the Congregationalist church at Whitchurch, his mother loved music and encouraged Edward's gift for it when he was a boy. Edward had a serious illness when he was sixteen which proved a blessing in disguise. The Joneses had three other children and were not well off, and his father wanted to apprentice Edward to an engineering firm; but when the boy recovered he was too old to be taken on. At this critical time Professor Walter Hay, conductor of the local Choral Society, saw Mr Jones and assured him Edward had the talent to get into the Royal Academy of Music, and offered to coach him. Edward passed in easily and won several medals and prizes at the Academy. He formed a strong friendship with Ethel Boyce, a piano student. His first symphony was performed in 1886, the same year that he composed *The Rival Poets,* a short operetta.

Having set out to be a composer, he changed his name to German to avoid being confused with other composers named Jones. He lived in London and earned very little money at first as subprofessor of the violin at the Royal Academy of Music. He also played second fiddle in a theatre orchestra, and sometimes deputised for a violinist at the Savoy Theatre. Edward German was hard up when he proposed to Ethel Boyce, who had been his sweetheart evr since they were students together. She wouldn't marry him unless he took up a more lucrative career, and she disapproved of the way he shut himself away like a hermit when he was composing. But German had already dedicated his life to music; he broke off the romance and resolved that no women would ever come before his work. Ethel Boyce wrote to him after he had sent her a copy of Herbert Scott's biography of him:

February 21, 1934.   The Orchard,
                                                                      Chertsey.

My dear German [his Christian name originally]

    . . . I like the little photograph I have of you in the light
suit better than any in the Book. I always wish we had seen
more of each other – as life drew on, you'd have realized how
country I really am, and that your hermit ways were also
mine, if possible.

153

...As you know, I *love* your music, and the certainty that it will remain is a comfort to me in this very ugly time.

And now, my dear Boy (for so you'll always be to me!) thank you again for the treasured book, and please believe in the continued affection of

Your old friend,

Ethel Boyce.[1]

Edward German got his first big chance when Richard Mansfield, the leading Shakesperean actor, engaged him as musical conductor at the Globe in 1888. Mansfield asked German to write incidental music for his production of *Richard III*; the critics gave his music splendid reviews when the play opened in March, 1891, and it made his reputation. Then Henry Irving commissioned him to write incidental music for his new production of *Henry VIII* at the Lyceum. He received 300 guineas for his work and was so surprised he thought Bram Stoker, Irving's manager, had made a mistake. German's *Henry VIII* music was acclaimed, and his 'Three Country Dances' from it became very popular and brought him world wide fame. Later, he wrote incidental music for the productions of Beerbohm Tree, Forbes Robertson and George Alexander.

In July, 1896, he moved to 5, Hall Road, a secluded house just off Maida Vale; it was surrounded by a high stone wall and its only door opened from the wall. German lived almost like a hermit in this bachelor retreat for the next twenty-five years. Sometimes the only woman he saw for weeks was his housekeeper. His principal relaxation was watching cricket at Lord's, which was only a few minutes away. But when he could fit in the time he went off on walking tours of the English countryside with Herbert Scott and other men friends, and every Christmas he returned to his family at Whitchurch.

After *The Emerald Isle* Helen D'Oyly Carte commissioned Edward German and Basil Hood to write another piece. Hood, knowing how German loved th English countryside and delighted in old English customs, wrote a libretto about Queen Elizabeth and her times

[1]Letter in the possession of Mrs Winifred German, Edward German's niece.

entitled *Merrie England*. Among the leading characters were the Earl of Essex and Sir Walter Raleigh, his rival for the Queen's favour. The comic opera, constructed on the lines of a masque, was an ideal subject for German to set to music; during 1901 he worked on the score with the greatest enthusiasm. The cast of *Merrie England* was almost the same as in *The Emerald Isle*: Rosina Brandram made a superb Queen Elizabeth, Robert Evett and Henry Lytton played Essex and Raleigh respectively, and Walter Passmore led the comics as an Elizabethan strolling player.

Produced at the Savoy on April 2, 1902, *Merrie England* had a wonderful reception and its success was a forgone conclusion, although Basil Hood was criticized for his heavy handed treatment of the plot. When the court is at Windsor Sir Walter Raleigh writes a secret love letter to Bessie Throckmorton, one of Queen Elizabeth's Maids of Honour. But his letter is mislaid and handed to his rival, the Earl of Essex, who shows it to Elizabeth. In a jealous rage the Queen puts Bessie Throckmorton in prison and banishes Raleigh. Bessie escapes to Windsor Forest, where the Earl of Essex turns up and is suddenly friendly towards her and Raleigh, being anxious for them to get married so that he can have Queen Elizabeth for himself. Essex devises a plan for a man to impersonate Herne the Hunter and 'appear' to Queen Elizabeth and frighten her out of her wits. The plan works and the terrified Queen pardons everybody, and Raleigh marries Bessie Throckmorton.

'Mr German shows so exquisite a sense of the lighter musical forms and is so accomplished a master of the orchestra that Sullivan's place seems to be vacant no more', said the *Pall Mall Gazette*. 'His success is not a repetition of the great original but, no less good, he may be described as his heir-at-music.' The *Times* conceded that German and Hood were well qualified to follow the tradition of Gilbert and Sullivan, 'but the mantles they have assumed are heavy ones . . . Compared with the exhilarating gaiety of its happiest predecessors, the new opera may possibly be found wanting in some rspects. But there will be none to say that *Merrie England* does not sustain the credit of a theatre where the best order of light music has had so long a hearing.'

The *Daily Telegraph* said, 'There is a wide difference between the requirements of the concert room and those of the light operatic stage, and even Mr German's experience as a writer of incidental music is not enough to bridge the gap...But Mr German goes his own way and indulges his own fancies with ample frequency...nothing can be more in his merit than the old world and rustic measures with which the piece is plentifully decked...the hornpipe, country dances or jigs are all equally delightful.'

German's score contained several very popular numbers, some of which are still sung to this day; amongst them were 'The Yeomen of England', 'She had a letter from her Love' the duet, 'When true love' and 'The English Rose'. 'The Yeomen of England' began:

Who were the Yeomen, the Yeomen of England?
The freemen were the Yeomen, the free men of England.
Stout were the bows they bore
When they went out to war,
Stouter their courage for the honour of England.

And nations to Eastward,
And nations to Westward,
As foemen did curse them,
The Bow-men of England,
No other land could nurse them,
But their Motherland, old England
And on her broad bosom did they ever thrive!

'The English Rose' is another ballad familiar to lovers of light music:

Dan Cupid hath a garden
Where women are the flowers
And lovers' laughs and lovers' tears,
The sunshine and the showers.
And oh! the sweetest blossom
That in the garden grows,
The fairest Queen, it is, I ween,
The perfect English rose.

Let others make a garland
Of every flow'r that blows!
But I will wait till I may pluck
My dainty English rose.
In perfume, grace and beauty
The rose doth stand apart,
God grant that I before I die
May wear one in my heart!

26. A cartoonist's impression of *Merrie England,* Edward German's comic opera
produced at the Savoy in 1901.

Merrie England had a successful season at the Savoy, and after a provincial tour it came back to London. While it was running, Edward German and Basil Hood wrote another piece, *A Princess of Kensington*. This fantasy about mixed-up fairies and mortals was so involved that when German first read Hood's libretto, he said: 'I doubt if anyone will know what this is about. I don't!' 'That's just it', Hood replied complacently, 'they will come again and try to find out.' It was unfortunate that German was such a nice man that he never seemed to quarrel with anybody; otherwise he might have put his foot down and insisted on Hood re-writing the 'book' to make it intelligible to the ordinary public.

Presented at the Savoy on January 23, 1903, *The Princess of Kensington* got some bad notices along with the good ones and came off fairly soon. The *Daily Telegraph* made odious comparisons between this fairy play and *Iolanthe*. 'To compare the opening of *The Princess of Kensington* and the first scene of *Iolanthe* is only to stress the irreplaceable loss British comic opera has sustained in the passing of Sir Arthur Sullivan, and there are many subsequent points in the play where the touch of a vanished hand would have brought in that order of humour in melody which Mr German lacks.'

The leading parts were again played by Walter Passmore, Henry Lytton and Robert Evett. The music included some charming numbers, of which the best was probably 'Seven o'clock in the morning'. The comparative failure of *The Princess of Kensington* upset Edward German very much; he was so sensitive about this setback that for the next two years he returned to composing serious music.

George Edwardes had presented an almost unbroken series of popular musical comedies at the Gaiety up till the new century. *The Toreador,* with Teddy Payne leading the fun and frolics, was still playing to packed houses when the London County Council ordered the theatre to be pulled down to make room for a new road scheme in the Strand. The last night of the old Gaiety on July 4, 1903, was an extremely nostalgic occasion; the public were queuing up all night to book the cheaper seats. Edwardes had invited Nellie Farren and other leading artistes from the burlesque period, and old John Hollingshead was also in the theatre. The valedictory speech was made by Sir Henry Irving, who had appeared on the Gaiety boards with J.L. Toole in *Uncle Dick's Darling* in 1869.

Sir Henry and George Edwardes had once been at loggerheads because Fred Leslie had done a devastating imitation of Irving in a Gaiety burlesque. Edwardes had therefore gone to see Irving at the Lyceum in the morning to make sure he was coming to the Gaiety to make his speech.

'The audience has been queuing up at the Gaiety for hours to see you this evening', said Edwardes diplomatically.

'Oh, really,' Irving replied.

'What's more, there isn't a vacant seat in the house tonight because the public know *you* are coming!'

'Hm – interesting,' drawled Irving. 'And I suppose the box office has been busy all day long just because I'm coming?'

'Oh yes, Sir Henry!'

'Edwardes, you're a damn liar!' cried Irving.[1]

The new Gaiety was built on the corner of the Strand and Aldwych, the new thoroughfare. Within a year bewitching Gertie Millar had become the new queen of the theatre. She had been discovered by Lionel Monckton, playing on tour in *The Messenger Boy*. This shy bachelor had fallen in love with her at first sight, but he had his work cut out to persuade the Guv'nor to bring her to London and give her a chance at the Gaiety. Monckton wrote her songs when she made her debut in *The Toreador* and stopped the show. The Guv'nor, realizing she had star quality, gave her a leading part in *The Orchid,* the first show at the new Gaiety. Before it opened there, Gertie Millar had married Lionel Monckton.

At Daly's *San Toy* had been followed by *A Country Girl*, an operetta with an English setting for a change. The score was by Lionel Monckton, the 'book' by James Tanner, and the lyrics by Adrian Ross and Percy Greenbank.

[1]The *Era* report of George Edwardes's speech to the O.P. Club, 1909.

27. Percy Greenbank, an outstanding lyrist for many years, contributed his first lyrics to *San Toy* when he was only twenty, taking over from his brother, the late Harry Greenbank.

When Harry Greenbank had to abandon his half-finished lyrics for *San Toy,* his twenty year old brother, Percy, had offered to finish them. (He had already started writing verses for *Punch*). He worked so well on *San Toy* that the Guv'nor put him under contract. The first time Percy Greenbank came to Daly's for a rehearsal he looked so young that a chorus girl called him 'the little boy in knickerbockers'. He contributed lyrics to many of Edwardes's most successful musical plays, amongst them *Our Miss Gibbs, The Quaker Girl, The Toreador, The Orchid, A Country Girl* and very many others.

In the new century Lionel Monckton, Paul Rubens and Howard Talbot wrote the music to many of his lyrics. Greenbank and Howard Talbot became great friends, and during the First World War they lived very near each other at Chalfont St Giles. Percy Greenbank found it hard to stick to regular working hours; he could only work to schedule if he had to meet a deadline. As soon as a show had been running a few months at the Gaiety or Daly's, the Guv'nor used to summon his team of composers and writers to his office and brief them on their work for the next piece. Greenbank loved pottering about in his garden at Aberdare Gardens, Hampstead, and never wanted to leave it unless he had to go and see the Guv'nor. In 1902 he married Hetty Pyne, whose father was head of Consols at the Bank of England. Greenbank was not a night bird in any sense of the word; after he had finished his work at the theatre, he would come straight home to his family.

For nearly two decades his world revolved round George Edwardes and his productions at the Gaiety, Daly's and elsewhere. He often wrote his lyrics sitting at the piano, and while he polished a lyric he used to rough out a tune for it. There were times when his passion for gardening caused him to get late with his lyrics. On one of these occasions Paul Rubens was moved to break into verse:

Hurry up, Percy, Percy hurry up,
Percy, hurry up do!
What is the matter, what is the matter with,
What is the matter with you?
I've been waiting for ages
For a lyric or two,

What a constipated muse you've got!
Mr Percy, hurry up do!

However, these random notes on Percy Greenbank have been a digression from Edwardes's production of *A Country Girl*.

George Edwardes had to cope with two catastrophes on the first night on January 18, 1902. A set which had been altered didn't arrive at the theatre till 9:00 – an hour after the curtain should have gone up – and the audience were getting most impatient. The Guv'nor took off his coat and helped the stage hands to get the new set into position. On top of that, Evie Greene, promoted to leading lady, had been so nervous that she took a strong drink on an empty stomach and had collapsed in her dressing room. When she recovered, the Guv'nor went in to see her and assured her the whole company was depending on her. Before the piece started he made an appropriate speech to the audience and, though *A Country Girl* went on till after midnight, the public forgave him and the piece ran for ages.

Lionel Monckton proved that he could write operettas just as well as musical comedies. 'Mr Monckton shows himself well equipped for a task demanding not merely a gay tune . . . but a goodly measure of musicianship as well', said the *Daily Telegraph*. The additional numbers, written by young Paul Rubens, were also praised. Evie Greene played Nan, a village beauty, and others in the strong cast included Hayden Coffin, Huntley Wright and Rutland Barrington. The performances of the principals and Lionel Monckton's score managed to offset a thin 'book' about a naval officer (Hayden Coffin) who comes home from sea to his Devon village to stand for Parliament, and gets involved with three different girls.

Outstanding numbers included the 'Rajah of Bhong', 'Yo ho, little girls' and 'Under the Deodar', which probably lasted longest of them all. It began:

Over the mountain passes,
Under the peaks of snow,
Forest and lawn, close to the dawn,
That is the land I know.
Meadows of waving grasses,

162

Wonderful woods above –
There would I be, over the sea,
There with the one I love.

Under the deodar,
Up in the hills afar,
Hearts may be lost,
Fates may be crossed,
Under the deodar.

Robert Courtneidge, after producing musical plays for George Edwardes when he first came to London, went into management on his own in 1905. Later, he and Alex Thompson wrote the 'book' of a comic opera, *Tom Jones,* based on Fielding's classic novel. Courtneidge commissioned Edward German to compose the score and Charles H. Taylor to write the lyrics. Courtneidge found German 'assiduous in rehearsal, conveying instruction and correction ... with the old-world courtesy that characterises his music'. *Tom Jones,* with Hayden Coffin in the name part, was presented at the Apollo on April 17, 1907, and received with enthusiasm.

The *Daily Mail* called it, 'A genuine comic opera that does credit to the London stage. Lovers of exquisite orchestration, of some admirable work that never stoops to the commonplace, will go again and again to the Apollo.' The *Daily Graphic* said, 'The audience positively revelled in the quaint grace of the madrigals and part-songs, sighed sympathetically over the graceful ballads and walked out of the theatre nodding their heads to the racy lilts of the Somersetshire ditties which are so delightful a feature of this work.' The *Tribune* went much further: 'It may be said that not since Sullivan left us has such new music been produced in an English opera.'

In the musical version of *Tom Jones* the amourous exploits of the lusty hero had, of course, been toned down. The story concentrated on the romance between Tom and Sophia Weston, the squire's daughter. Sophia falls in love with penniless Tom Jones after he has rescued her and refuses to obey her father and marry Blifil, the ghastly nephew of wealthy Mr Allworthy. Tom is in love with Sophia but, feeling there is no hope for him, he runs away from his Somerset village. On the road to London he rescues Lady Belaston from highwaymen, and in return she does her best to inveigle him into her bed at an inn. Sophia, who has run away from home, turns up at the inn and concludes that Tom has deserted her for Lady Belaston. In the last act, at Ranelagh Gardens, Tom and Sophia are re-united after it has been discovered that Tom Jones, the foundling, is really Mr Allworthy's nephew and heir.

Hayden Coffin and Ruth Vincent, playing Tom Jones and Sophia, were both in fine voice and carried off the honours of the evening. The best numbers in Edward German's score included 'West Country Lad', 'The Green Ribbon', 'I Wonder', 'The Barley Mow' and 'If Love's Content'. The latter was sung by Hayden Coffin:

If Love's content lies in the spoken word,
Then must more accomplished tongue than mine
Be eloquent and I remain unheard.
Where facile wit o'er humbler gifts doth shine,
I have no wealth of words – no courtier's art,
With store of money'd speech my love to greet;
And can no more than bring a beating heart,
And, asking nothing, lay it at her feet.
Come, then, fortune or ill befall,
Go Heart, wavering never;
And if she deem the offering small,
Yet I will love her ever.
Come, then, happiness or despair,
It asketh nothing but to live and die for her.

Robert Courtneidge arranged for *Tom Jones* to be presented in New York by Colonel Savage, and went over to the States with Edward German to supervise the production. *Tom Jones* had a moderate success, but never had the same appeal for Americans as *H.M.S. Pinafore* or *The Mikado* or *The Gondoliers*. German was interviewed by the *Boston Transcript,* which reported: 'Not at all the rollicking author of comic scores seemed this prim, neatly-dressed little man, with the suggestion of an academic in his manner. But you

28. Tom Jones (Hayden Coffin) is finally re-united with his true love, Sophia (Ruth Vincent) with some help from the jealous Lady Bellaston. Edward German's second outstanding comic opera appeared at the Lyric in 1907.

instantly liked the clear, unaffected English of his speech...'

In the new century W.S. Gilbert had been knighted at last for his services to the drama. Encouraged by the success of the Gilbert and Sullivan revivals he had produced for Helen D'Oyly Carte at the Savoy, the seventy year old author wrote a libretto in 1908 and looked around for a composer to set it to music. His piece, based on his old play, *The Wicked World,* was turned down by Sir Edward Elgar, Andre Messager and Sir Alexander Mackenzie. Then Gilbert sent a copy to Edward German, who agreed to undertake the score. Flattered by the prospect of collaborating with Gilbert, German failed to realize that he would have to set a sub-standard libretto. Gilbert wrote to him:

Grim's Dyke,
    Harrow Weald.   17th February, 1909.

Dear German,
    I was very glad you find the work interesting and I hope you will pull it about, alter and reconstruct the numbers to suit your music.

165

German mentioned the piece in a letter to his sister, Rachel, that summer:

> ... I have now finished the first act ... Gilbert seems very pleased with it; still I, personally and privately, have little faith in it for running purposes ... Gilbert is delightful to work with ... The fact is he is such a giant that he can afford to be doubly polite and nice.

Gilbert called his new piece *Fallen Fairies*. One great flaw was that there was no male chorus and all the choral singing had been given to the fairies. The second, of course, was that it had a weak libretto. *Fallen Fairies* was presented by a syndicate headed by Charles Workman, the new Gilbert and Sullivan star. To make matters worse, Gilbert forced the syndicate to engage his protegée, Nancy McIntosh, as leading lady – although it was fifteen years since she had played in *Utopia Ltd*. Gilbert was told that one of the syndicate had put up £1,000 on the understanding that Elsie Spain should play the leading female role, but he vetoed the suggestion.

Fallen Fairies was presented at the Savoy on October 15, 1909 with Charles Workman and Nancy McIntosh in the principal parts. The action takes place in a fairyland inhabited only by female sprites, who summon two 'barbaric' males to their paradise in order to reform them. But instead of that the two fairies fall in love with them. The *Daily Mail* said, 'The author's hallmark was on all the lyrics ... even if it cannot be pretended that he has always sharpened his pencil in this instance to its finest point.' The same critic remarked that Nancy McIntosh's 'voice is no longer remarkable for its freshness.' Charles Workman laboured in vain to build up his part of Lutin, a fairy with a male counterpart.

The word went round that *Fallen Fairies* had misfired, and it did very badly in its first week. Workman's syndicate panicked and dismissed Nancy McIntosh for incompetence. Gilbert flew into a terrible rage and started an action against Workman, calling on Edward German to support him. German, who hated disputes just as much as Sullivan, promised to back up Gilbert, but one can read between the lines in his letter:

5, Hall Road,
St. John's Wood, N.W.

Dear Sir William,

Yes, I will go with you to your Solicitors tomorrow
morning as you suggest, but I cannot, as you know,
conscientiously say to him that the singing of Miss McIntosh
has quite come up to my expectations. Her artistic attributes
generally are so strong that I am prepared to sign an
affidavit to the effect that we are satisfied that she should
play the part.

Yours very truly,

E.G.

P.S.   I must add that the action of the syndicate in
dismissing Miss McIntosh as they did is intolerable,
and of course violates our contract with them.

But *Fallen Fairies* – with or without Nancy McIntosh – was
doomed to failure. It was taken off at the end of January and Gilbert
decided to call off his law suit against Workman. One feels bound to
quote this interesting letter on the subject, written by Sir Alexander
Mackenzie to his great friend, Edward German:

Sunday 16/1/10   6, Abbey Court,
                                        Abbey Road, N.W.

My dear Edward,

I suppose you have heard that the 'notice' is up on the
call-board, terminating the run of *Fallen Fairies* in a
fortnight? My sympathies are entirely with you, in the whole
wretched and unhappy history of the piece up to now.

And I can't help saying that I think Gilbert has acted,
and is acting, in a manner so inconsiderate as to be
contemptuous of you and the deservedly very high position
which you occupy in the musical world of this country.

On the occasion of his speech after the first night he

167

spoke of there being 'life in the old dog yet'. The sort of life he exhibits, as an unwholesome old hound, is not edifying.

As ever,
Yours,

A. Mac.[1]

After the dismal failure of *Fallen Fairies,* and the various embarrassments connected with its production, Edward German never wrote another comic opera or composed any other kind of work for the thatre. In 1912 he turned down an offer from Sir Herbert Tree to write a special score for his production of *Drake* at His Majesty's. The hermit of Maida Vale, who had once been a hot favourite to assume the mantle of Sullivan, had been so upset by his collaboration with Gilbert that it was his last experience in the theatre.

[1]Letter in the possession of Mrs Winifred German.

CHAPTER FOURTEEN

THE FLORODORA MAN

Leslie Stuart – A son of Lancashire who moved the nation to song

FROM A MEMORIAL PLAQUE IN MANCHESTER PUBLIC LIBRARY

'Florodora' was an intoxicating perfume named after the South Sea Island where it was distilled in the greatest secrecy. This perfume was the mainspring of one of the most popular musical plays of the 'nineties, written by Owen Hall, the author of *The Geisha*. *Florodora*, produced at the Lyric on November 11, 1899, by Tom Davis, made a fortune for its composer, Leslie Stuart, who had started life in a humble way at Southport. Leslie Stuart also wrote popular songs like 'Lily of Languna' and 'Little Dolly Daydreams', which were sung on the halls by Eugene Stratton, the black-faced American, and had composed 'Soldiers of the Queen', the unofficial National Anthem at the end of the century when British soldiers were fighting the Boers in South Africa.

The plot of *Florodora* was unabashed melodrama: the secret formula of the perfume is stolen from Dolores, the hard-working heroine, by the wicked proprietor of the South Sea Island. But after Dolores has recovered the formula of the perfume in England, she can afford to marry the man she loves and all ends happily. Nobody cared a hang about the plot when Willy Edouin, the principal comedian, appeared and started to feel everybody's bumps in his role of a phoney phrenologist. Edouin's half-shaven moustache, his Welsh harp, and his grotesque gyrations were quite sufficient to keep the audience entertained for an hour.

The *Daily Telegraph* said: 'A fine cast of popular people, mounting that delighted the eye and rejoiced the heart, music which was never dull... together with uproariously mirthful snatches of acting, soon made certain that *Florodora* was in for a good time.

169

Florodora, from the opening chorus to the closing numbers, bears evidence of a clever and tuneful facility . . . Mr Stuart keeps our fingers thrumming and our heads wagging.' Another critic summed up *Florodora* unkindly as 'this piece of Surrey melodrama, served up with Lyric sauce, and dashed with suggestions of *Carmen* and *The Sorcerer.'*

However, there was never any doubt of its success, thanks mainly to Leslie Stuart's score and the comic acting of Willy Edouin. Evie Greene received excellent notices for her performance as Dolores, the heroine, and so did Ada Reeve, playing a caricature of a titled lady. 'Tact', sung by Ada Reeve, was one of the most popular songs, but the best number in the piece was 'Tell me, Pretty Maiden'. This original sextet for girls and men is still held in high esteem; 'any superior person who does not promptly succumb to its enchantment should be made to copy it out bar by bar', said Gervase Hughes, the critic:

Men: Tell me, pretty maiden,
        Are there any more at home like you?
Girls: There are a few, kind sir,
        But simple girls and proper too.
Men: Then tell me, pretty maiden
        What these very simple girlies do.
Girls: Kind sir, their manners are perfection
        And the opposite of mine.
Men: Then tell me, maiden, what the girlies do,
        Then take a little walk with me,
        And then I can see
        What a most particular girl should be.
Girls: I may love you too well to let you go
        And flirt with those at home, you know.
Men: Well, don't mind, little girl, you'll see
        I'll only want but you.
Girls: It's not quite fair to them

29. Leslie Stuart became the most popular song writer of the day with numbers like 'Lily of Laguna' and 'Soldiers of the Queen'. He wrote the immensely popular musical play, *Florodora,* in 1899, but never repeated his success. ▷

                If you told them that you were true.
    Men: I don't care a pin for your sisters if you love me.
    Girls: What would you say if I said I liked you well?
    Men: I'd vow to you –
    Girls: On bended knee!
    Men: On bended knee!
    Girls: If I loved you,
                Would you tell me what I ought to do
                To keep you all mine alone
                To always be true to me?
                If I loved you,
                Would it be a silly thing to do?
                For I must love someone.
    Men: Then why not me?
    Girls: Yes, I must love someone really,
                And it might as well be you!

Florodora had a wonderful run of eighteen months; its popularity endured till the last night, and Leslie Stuart received royalties in the region of £300 a week. This sudden shower of wealth had a fatal effect on a man who had never seen such sums of money in his life. He bought a mansion in Hampstead and entertained like a millionaire, drinking champagne for breakfast like the notorious Horatio Bottonley. The fact that he was married didn't stop him behaving like a playboy. Fair, good looking and with charming manners, he often popped into the Gaiety and took out a bevy of girls to lunch or to supper. For the next decade Leslie Stuart lived like a Rajah, and lost a lot of money gambling on horseraces and cards.

He had been born Thomas Augustus Barrett at Southport on March 15, 1866. His father was property master at a theatre in Liverpool where his mother, an actress, often appeared on the boards. When both his parents were working at the theatre, baby Tom used to sit on the stage on a sugar box. As a young boy he already showed a talent for music, and left school at fifteen to become an organist at St John's Roman Catholic Cathedral, Salford. He earned extra money giving music lessons and composing church music and also tried his hand at writing popular ballads, but couldn't sell them. In 1888 he became organist at the church of the Holy Name, Manchester, and continued to write popular songs which nobody wanted to buy.

At that time the only way for an unknown composer to make a success with a song was to persuade a big star to sing it. After selling 'The Bandalero' to Signor Foli, Tom Barrett heard that Ada Reeve was coming to the Princes' Theatre, Manchester. When he played her 'Louisiana Lou', she liked it so much that she sang it in 'The Shop Girl' at the Gaiety. Though Barrett only got a few guineas for the song, he was so encouraged that he came to London to try and make his fortune; the first thing he did was to change his name to Leslie Stuart.

In the 'nineties Stuart wrote dozens of songs for Eugene Stratton to sing on the halls. Stratton used to sing 'Lily of Laguna' with his face blacked and would end the number by performing his inimitable soft-shoe dance. 'Lily of Laguna', 'Little Dolly Daydreams', 'The Little Octoroon' and other songs by Stuart were played all over Britain, but there was a catch in it: he only received a few guineas for each song, but Eugene Stratton sang them on the halls at a salary of £200 a week.

Florodora completely changed the world of Leslie Stuart; in the first years of the new century he was inundated with commissions to write scores for musical plays. He went on wild spending sprees and, having no idea of the value of money, rashly assumed that it would be easy to write a few more *Florodoras*. Although he never wrote another piece to compare with it, he continued living it up as if he had a private gold mine.

Leslie Stuart and Owen Hall collaborated again on *The Silver Slipper,* an extravaganza produced at the Lyric on June 1, 1901. It begins when Stella, a lovely young lady of Venus, kicks off her slipper, which falls all the way down to earth. Her planetary friends persuade her to go and retrieve it, which brings the action to London. Stella's beauty breaks up a girl's romance, then the inconsequential plot goes to Paris.

The Silver Slipper had a good reception, but some of the notices criticized Stuart's music. The *Daily Mail* said:

Like all composers who have arrived at a particular order of success ... Mr Leslie

173

30. The charming Ada Reeve as Lady Holyrood in *Florodora*, produced at the Lyric in 1899. She stopped the show with her number, 'Tact'.

Stuart challenges comparison between his new work and what has gone before. The music of *Florodora* contains so many elements of gaiety and grace that it could hardly be surpassed in these respects . . . Here the composer's tunes romp merrily along, giving the ear a hard time to keep pace with their tricks and turns. He revels in a complicated measure and a 'prolonged cadence' is to him the breath of life . . . All will remember the delightful 'Tell me, Pretty Maiden' in *Florodora* with its quaint, irregular rhythm . . . but its success has led the composer to work his devices a little too hard . . . but many numbers catch the ear very pleasantly . . .

Willie Edouin starred as a highly disreputable riding master, and

31. Edna May, the enormously popular American star, in *The Belle of Mayfair,* a musical play composed by Leslie Stuart and produced at the Vaudeville in 1906.

shared the best notices with Connie Ediss, the comedienne. 'Class', a comic ditty sung by Connie Ediss, was the most popular number in the piece. Though *The Silver Slipper* had a disappointing run, Leslie Stuart still drank champagne for breakfast and wagered heavily on horses which often finished down the course. Sometimes he went racing with Eugene Stratton, the music hall star who had made his songs famous. But one day they had a row at Hurst Park about the merits of a certain filly; Stuart walked off in a huff and refused to speak to Stratton again for many years. A crony of George Edwardes, Stuart used to play cards regularly in his office at the Gaiety; the games went on all night and they played for high stakes.

Leslie Stuart next wrote the music of *The School Girl,* starring Edna May, which George Edwardes presented at the Prince of Wales's on May 9, 1903. Edna May, the American star of *The Belle of New York,* had such a big following that her appearance in a piece could almost guarantee its success. *The School Girl* was not an outstanding operetta, but it ran for over 330 performances. The story starts in a convent where Cicely Marchant, a General's daughter, is on the eve of getting married off to a man about town she doesn't love. Lilian, her best friend, runs away from the convent to Paris, where she believes she can help Cicely to come to an understanding with the artist she really loves. She exposes a bogus gold mine at the Open Exchange and the two girls have a good time at a masquerade ball, after which all ends happily. The *Era* said: 'Seldom has the virginal style of Edna May been so effective as in her rendering of the part of Lilian.' Her best numbers were 'Call round again' and 'Clytie'. Marie Studholme played Cicely and had a delightful number, 'The Honeymoon Girl'. The principal comedians were G.P. Huntley, who played the man about town and made a hit with his number 'Belinda'; and George Graves, who played General Marchant.

The Belle of Mayfair, with music by Leslie Stuart and a 'book' by Charles Brookfield and Cosmo Hamilton, was presented at the Vaudeville on April 11, 1906; like *The School Girl,* it provided a vehicle for Edna May, and had a long run of 400 performances. The *Daily News* said:

The popularity of Miss Edna May can easily be accounted for. Miss May's appearance is angelic, and her style is calm and virginal . . . She has the invaluable stage asset, a distinct individualtiy . . . the combination of a West End manner and an eastern American accent is all that can be of bewitching . . . *The Belle of Mayfair* is clear, bright and pretty all through – just the kind of 'show' to which ordinary people resort to look upon tasteful costumes, to listen to lively and agreeable airs, and to enjoy the efforts of favourite artists.

Louie Pounds had two popular numbers, 'Said I to myself, said I' and 'The Weeping Willow wept', and Courtice Pounds, her brother, scored in a comedy number which compared marriage to a ride in one of the new-fangled motor cars. Stuart's music was praised by the *Daily News*: 'It lilts, it lifts, and falls, and it enlivens and it amuses – all in the same elegant, artless, irresponsible way.'

Next year George Edwardes commissioned Stuart to write *Havana* to follow *The Merry Widow* at Daly's. Edwardes never expected Lehar's operetta to run for long, but *The Merry Widow* created a furore and ran for ages. The Guv'nor therefore put on *Havana* at the Gaiety in order to keep the cast together. It starred Evie Greene and Alfred Lester, whose gloomy expression was his trademark, and had a bad start. The Gaiety patrons, conditioned to the free-and-easy style of musical comedy, found *Havana* slow and much too mild for them. To strengthen the piece, Edwardes brought in W.H. Berry. Big Bill Berry, one of the most cheerful comedians of his period, made a perfect contrast to the lugubrious Alfred Lester. But when Bill Berry began to get more laughs than Alfred Lester, and took over his number, 'Filibuster Brown', Lester got very jealous and demanded to see the Guv'nor one night after the show.

George Edwardes, who was playing cards in his office with Walter Pallant, the Gaiety chairman, Leslie Stuart and others, said to them: 'Now for the love of Mike don't mention the name of Bill Berry to Lester! It might slip out, but if it does it'll be like a red rag to a bull!' Alfred Lester came into the office looking the picture of misery. Edwardes got up from the table, beamed at him and said, 'Hello Berry, how are you?' After that it took all the Guv'nor's well known tact to calm down the infuriated comedian.

Sidney Jones, having severed his connection with Daly's, wrote the scores of *My Lady Molly* and *See-See. My Lady Molly* had a good run, *See-See* only a fair one, but neither of these pieces enhanced his reputation. He wrote one of his best scores for *The King of Cadonia,* an operetta presented by Frank Curzon at the Prince of Wales's on September 3, 1908, which ran for 330 performances. Adrian Ross had written the lyrics and Frederick Lonsdale, a new author, wrote the 'book'.

The *Daily Telegraph* called *The King of Cadonia,* an excellent specimen of what a musical play should be, bright, tuneful, cheery and entertaining . . . Frederick Lonsdale's work is distinguished by a vivacity, a neatness and an ample sense of humour which should serve him well in the future . . . in the score of *The King of Cadonia* Mr Sidney Jones displays the same breadth of style, the same fund of tunefulness, the same mastery of his subject that he has shown in previous works. . . His score has a dainty touch that gives to everything he does an added charm, while in the big numbers he shows a strength and resource that serve to dominate the situations.

The King of Cadonia had a Ruritanian plot about a monarch who roams about his kingdom in disguise, like Haroun el Raschid, and happens to fall in love with a girl who turns out to be the Princess he is supposed to marry. Bertram Wallis – the successor to Hayden Coffin – and Isabel Jay sang well and acted magnificently in the principal roles. Huntley Wright as an exceedingly timid Duke brought the house down with his number, 'Do not Hesitate to Shoot'. 'There is a King in the land to-day', sung by Bertram Wallis, was another outstanding number. Several critics praised the lyrics by Adrian Ross – 'his lyrics are quite up to the level of that witty writer's standard; no higher praise could be given them.'

George Edwardes decided he needed another theatre in addition to the Gaiety and Daly's for the production of his musical plays. Believing that three theatres would give him a better chance to break even on his very expensive productions, he took over the Adelphi. He made a wonderful start on November 5 with *The Quaker Girl*, which co-starred Gertie Millar and Joe Coyne fresh from his triumph in *The Merry Widow*. Lionel Monckton composed the outstanding score, James Tanner wrote the 'book' and Adrian Ross and Percy Greenbank the lyrics. '*The Quaker Girl* promises to be as successful as any of Mr George Edwardes's productions at the Gaiety and Daly's' said the *Era*. 'There is no reason why, after its baptism of comic opera...the Adelphi need not become the home of light, pretty, frivolous and dainty entertainment.'

Gertie Millar had the part of a lifetime as Prudence Pym, the Quaker girl, who is persuaded by a charming American diplomat (Joe Coyne) and a French dressmaker to walk out on her puritanical family and go to Paris to model the new Quaker fashions. 'Miss Gertie Millar's quaint and peculiar charms have never been more vividly displayed', said the *Era*. 'She renders her musical numbers in her original and artistic way . . . There was something elusively fascinating about Miss Millar's rendering of the role, and her dancing was delightful . . . Mr Joe Coyne's engaging and very graceful and resourceful performance as the scapegrace lover, Tony Chute, won the hearts of the audience completely so full was it of vitality, gaiety and pleasant assurance.'

Of the music the critic said, 'Mr Lionel Monckton . . . has seldom been more happily inspired than in the score of *The Quaker Girl*, which is more musicianly and coherent than several of his past achievements.' The *Daily Chronicle* was enraptured: 'A beautiful theatre, a beautiful production, with taste in every frill of the costumier and every fancy of the scenic painter . . . Most important of all, there is Miss Gertie Millar as *The Quaker Girl* herself. It is, of

32. Gertie Millar as Prudence is taught how to dance by Tony from America (Joe
    Coyne) in *The Quaker Girl,* produced by George Edwardes at the Adelphi in
    1910.

course, the daintiness, neatness and perpetual intelligence of this
artist that is at the heart of the whole escapade...'

The hits included 'A Quaker Girl', Gettie Millar and Joe Coyne's
duets, 'A Dancing Lesson' and 'The bad boy and the good girl', and
'Just as Father used to do'. 'Come to the Ball', the most popular
number of all, was sung by a French prince to the Quaker Girl (Gertie
Millar) on whom he has designs:

Will you not come to the ball?

Listen and answer the call?
Beautiful girls will be there to dance
All that is fairest and best in France!
If you will come to the ball
You shall be queen of them all,
For no one so fair will be there
At the ball – at the ball!

When Gertie Millar left the Gaiety for the Adelphi, George Edwardes needed a leading lady to replace her; but it was almost impossible to find anybody to match her appeal. He chose Phyllis Dare, a very pretty actress who could sing and dance charmingly; but her unsophisticated manner didn't quite get over at the Gaiety, whose patrons had idolized Gertie Millar for her vivacity and her little hint of sauciness. Leslie Stuart composed the score of *Peggy,* which starred Phyllis Dare at the Gaiety on March 4, 1911. But his music was too slow and subtle for that theatre and, although Teddy Payne and George Grossmith worked like Trojans in support of Phyllis Dare, *Peggy* came off after 270 performances and lost money.

The critics complained that Leslie Stuart had only repeated himself in the score of *Peggy*; several of his numbers with very intricate rhythms sounded as if they were discarded versions of 'Tell me, Pretty Maiden'. Theatre people considered *Florodora* far and away the best thing he had ever done, and the theatre gossips began saying that Leslie Stuart had had his day. He carried on gambling and painting the town red in his old way until there was no money left in the bank to meet his commitments. Creditors began to dun Leslie Stuart for their bills and he was forced to sell his London house.

The craze for ragtime music came over from America after 1911, and jazz soon followed it to England. Stuart's slow and melodious kind of music became old-fashioned almost in a night. And the rumour went round that the man who had once been the most popular song writer in the country was on the brink of bankruptcy. At this crucial point I shall leave Leslie Stuart, with his future a big question mark, and in the next chapter trace the careers of two other leading composers.

CHAPTER FIFTEEN

TWO OF THE BEST

We have seldom had the pleasure of playing under a conductor whom we esteem so highly.

THE ORCHESTRA OF *MONTE CARLO'S* TRIBUTE TO *HOWARD TALBOT*

He was generosity itself, and charming to all the world – a gentleman in the truest and most delicate sense of the word.

WILLIAM BOOSEY ABOUT *PAUL RUBENS*

When Howard Munkittrick, a medical student, fainted at his first sight of blood at King's College Hospital, it confirmed that he was not cut out to be a doctor. He had set his heart on becoming a musician but his father, Alexander Munkittrick, a pillar of the insurance world, thought music a very bad risk and had forced him to take a medical degree. After this experience, Howard was apprenticed to a silk merchant and disliked it just as much as working in a hospital. Coming into some money at twenty one, he enrolled himself at the Royal College of Music and paid his own fees. He had once been the apple of his father's eye, but when Alexander Munkittrick heard that he had thrown up a secure future for music he summoned the youth to his study and told him: 'You can live in my house, but you are no longer a son of mine!' Howard continued to live at home, although his father would never speak to him; but he kept on good terms with his mother, and at her suggestion changed his name to her maiden name of Talbot.

This testimonial from Sir Hubert Parry of the Royal College of Music ought to have made both his parents proud of him:

17 Kensington Square, W.   June 20, 1890

I have great pleasure in giving my testimony to the exceptional musical abilities of Mr Howard Talbot. I believe him to be thoroughly at home in matters of Musical Theory, and to have a very competent knowledge of Orchestration, as well as skill and facility in composition.

C. Hubert Parry.

33. Howard Talbot, Irish composer of the record breaking *Chinese Honeymoon*, wrote several successful musical plays afterwards and collaborated with Lionel Monckton on the score of *The Arcadians* in 1909.

Howard Talbot wrote his first music to accompany the Swedish Drill Company. He had the music proofs in his pocket when Alexander Munkittrick sent for him again. 'If by any chance you ever do get anything published, you do not use my name!' ordered his stern parent. Talbot had the pleasure of taking the proofs from his pocket and laying them before Munkittrick, showing the composer's name to be Howard Talbot. He said, 'You needn't worry, Father, I have not!' The old man never forgot it.

Talbot's first important composition, a cantata entitled *A Musical Chess Tournament*, was performed by the King's Lynn Choral Society and at Oxford. While at King's Lynn, Howard Talbot made friends with Arthur Cross, organist at the Royal Chapel at Sandringham. And he made such a good impression on the choral society that they arranged to produce his first operetta, *Wapping Old Stairs*, composed under the influence of Arthur Sullivan. The *Times* critic wrote: 'Of the music of Mr Howard Talbot, it is our pleasure to speak in terms of almost unqualified praise.' *Wapping Old Stairs* was produced at the Vaudeville on February 17, 1894, with a strong cast headed by three Savoyards – Courtice Pounds, Jessie Bond and Richard Temple. The *Daily Telegraph* hurled brickbats at the 'book', but added: 'We see no reason to regret the new play's coming since it has introduced to us a young composer who knows how to give bright and engaging melody the true musicianly air.'

Wapping Old Stairs was bogged down by a melodramatic plot which centred round the efforts of a sailor in the eighteenth century to clear himself of a murder for which he has been framed by a deep-dyed villain. He spends most of the time playing hide and seek with the police, only returning to claim his sweetheart in the last act. Though the piece only ran a few weeks, it had brought Howard Talbot's name to the notice of the public and given him a start in his career.

Monte Carlo, his second comic opera, produced at the Avenue on August 27, 1896, fared no better. But at least Talbot had the satisfaction of conducting his own work. He was most touched when the orchestra gave him a small present on the last night – November 6 – and their leader, Reginald Creake, made the following speech:

Mr Talbot,

As this is, unfortunately, our final programme, the 'boys' have asked me to say a few words of thanks to you for the unvarying kindness with which we have been treated during the run of *Monte Carlo* ...

We are all of us 'old stagers' ... But I am sure they will agree with me when I say that in the whole course of our experience it has seldom been, if ever, that we have had the pleasure of playing under a Conductor whom we esteem so highly . . . So far as I have heard there has not been an angry word spoken anywhere in the theatre, either at rehearsal or performance. And the 'boys' in the orchestra wish to show their appreciation of this happy state of affairs, first of all by asking you to accept their heartfelt thanks, and, after that, as an assurance of their high esteem for you both as a Composer and a Conductor, to ask you to accept a small present which I now have the pleasure of handing over to you.

We shall always think with pleasure of the good time we had with you in *Monte Carlo*.[1]

Howard Talbot, who was Irish on both sides, had a strong belief in his luck; it was certainly third time lucky when he wrote the score of *A Chinese Honeymoon*. George Dance, the librettist, had written a wonderful comedy part for Louie Frear as an eccentric Cockney waitress in a Chinese restaurant. A great deal of fun arose from an old Chinese custom which said that the kiss of a royal personage amounts to an act of betrothal; it caused great embarrassment to both the Emperor of China and one of the Princesses. After *A Chinese Honeymoon* had been very popular in the provinces, Frank Curzon presented it on October 7, 1901, at the Strand where it had an excellent reception.

The *Daily Telegraph* singled out Louie Frear's performance: 'Miss Louie Frear made a quick appeal, not only on her native sense of fun, but also in a group of songs written "round her" . . . it says much for the player's skill that she "lets herself go" without offending . . . Mr Howard Talbot's music is just what it should be – tuneful and not unduly ambitious. His melodies and rhythms are clear cut . . . While, when opportunity offers, the hand of the practical musician appears with excellent effect.'

Louie Frear had a monopoly of the outstanding numbers in the piece, such as 'I want to be a Lidy', 'The Twiddly Bits' and 'Click, Click', her duet with the Emperor of China. Her biggest hit was 'Martha

[1]Howard Talbot papers, Victoria and Albert Museum.

34. The life and soul of *A Chinese Honeymoon* (Strand, 1899) was Louie Frear as Fi-Fi, a waitress in a Chinese restaurant. She brought the house down with her comedy numbers and innumerable disguises.

spanks the grand pianner', which conjures up a picture of the home-made music of the period; Victorians used to invite their friends to dinner and tell them 'be sure to bring your music'. This was the chorus:

> And Martha spanks the grand pianner,
> Father whacks the drum;

35. A scene from *The Arcadians* after Simplicitas/Smith (Dan Rolyat) has won the big race at Askwood with the help of the Arcadians. Produced by Robert Courtneidge at the Shaftesbury, the piece ran for over 800 performances.

> Mother in a soulful manner
> Blows the tootle-tum.
> Charlie swings the concertina,
> Bob goes fiddle-de-dee;
> And I'm a brick, for I waggle the stick
> With a one, two three.

The indefatigable Louis Frear and the exotic settings – inspired by the previous successes of *The Mikado* and *San Toy* – made the success of *A Chinese Honeymoon*; it had a phenomenal run of 1,076 performances, a record for a musical play at the time. Howard Talbot, brought up in a middle class home, didn't let success turn his head. In 1904 George Edwardes engaged him to conduct the orchestra at the Prince of Wales's, a job he was able to combine with composition. He collaborated with Paul Rubens on the score of *The Blue Moon,* which Robert Courtneidge presented at the Lyric on August 28, 1905. *The*

Blue Moon only had a fair run, its chances being wrecked by a particularly silly 'book'. The talented cast included Florence Smithson, who had a lovely singing voice, Willie Edouin, Courtice Pounds and Walter Passmore.

Howard Talbot's next piece, *The Belle of Brittany*, was presented at the Queen's on October 24, 1908. Ruth Vincent, the heroine of *Tom Jones*, played the beauty who toils all day on a daffodil farm in Britanny. The sugary story ends with her marrying the man she loves and doing her best to shower happiness on all the characters. George Graves, the comedian, played a ridiculous French Marquis and had to work terribly hard to get laughs. Howard Talbot's music was called 'light, lively and refined', but the piece only had a moderate success.

In 1909 Talbot and Lionel Monckton collaborated on the score of *The Arcadians*, one of the best operettas of the Edwardian period. The two composers tossed up as to whose name should appear first on the programme and Monckton won. (It seems amazing that, even in this year of grace, the BBC sometimes gives the impression that Lionel Monckton wrote *The Arcadians* on his own.) The charming book was by Mark Ambient and A.M. Thomson and the delightful lyrics by Arthur Wimperis. Yet when Robert Courtneidge presented *The Arcadians* at the Shaftesbury on April 28, he was almost the only man in England who believed the fantasy would be a success. This story of fairies and mortals appealed immensely to the public; the production never faltered and it thoroughly deserved the long run of 809 performances.

'There is something of Gilbert's topsy-turvydom in the book', said the *Era*, 'and it is all delightful, exhiliarating, picturesque and a very riot of drollery.' It begins in Arcady, where the carefree inhabitants are shocked when James Smith, a middle-aged caterer, lands there from his 'plane. After being purified and re-juvenated in the Well of Truth, Smith is transformed into Simplicitas, a shepherd, and sent back to earth with Sombra and Chrysea, two delectable Arcadians, to go and convert the wicked Londoners to the simple life.

Simplicitas Smith, thanks to his new powers, rides a wild racehorse to victory in the big race at Askwood for Jack Meadows. Then he and the Arcadian girls start an Arcadian restaurant, assisted

187

by Peter Doody, a melancholy jockey who has never won a race. Sombra innocently captivates all the male visitors to the restaurant, and Simplicitas/Smith gets his head turned when he is lionized, and makes a fool of his unsuspecting wife, Mrs Smith. Sombra brings about the engagement of Jack Meadows and Eileen, his Irish sweetheart, Simplicitas changes back into Smith, and the Arcadian maidens decide to return home.

'The excellent comedians, with methods that are in admirable contrast, keep the fun going from first to last', said the *Era*. 'Mr Dan Rolyat as Simplicitas/Smith had the house swaying with laughter. He has an excellent foil in Miss Ada Blanche as his wife . . . Mr Alfred Lester's monologue as the jockey who has never won a race is distinctly precious and the comedian preserves that lugubrious expression which makes his song, "I've got a motter, always merry and bright" so strikingly whimsical.'

Florence Smithson as Sombra was complimented on her lovely singing of 'The Pipes of Pan', 'Arcady is every young' and 'Light is my Heart', and Phyllis Dare scored as the Irish heroine. Lionel Monckton wrote many popular numbers in the piece, while Howard Talbot wrote "My Motter" and the choruses. 'The Pipes of Pan' began:

> With a melody enthralling
> Loud the woodland echoes ring.
> Hark! the pipes of Pan are calling
> With a merry lilt and swing.
> Hear their joyous carolling,
> Flowing, growing, rising, falling
> Youth and joy must have their fling
> When the pipes of Pan are calling –
> Ah! the pipes of Pan,
> So follow, follow, follow!

Alfred Lester sang "My Motter", looking a picture of gloom; his ditty has probably had a longer life than any other number in the piece.

> I've got a motter
> Always merry and bright!

Look around and you will find
Every cloud is silver-lined.
The sun will shine
Although the cloud's a grey one.
I've often said to myself, I've said,
'Cheer up, Cully, you'll soon be dead!'
A short life and a gay one!

While *The Arcadians* was still on, Howard Talbot accompanied Robert Courtneidge and his wife on a trip to Japan via the Trans-Siberian Railway. They toured Japan to get atmosphere for *The Mousmé*, the next Courtneidge production, and then returned to England by sea. Talbot had fallen in love with Dorothy Cross, the daughter of his friend Arthur Cross, the organist at Sandringham. Their romance had started after Cross had asked Talbot to act as guardian to Dorothy when she came to London to train as an actress at RADA. Dorothy Cross, a lovely girl twenty years younger than Howard Talbot, accepted his proposal while he was still in the Far East; he hurried home and married her on January 1, 1910. Dorothy, who had acted under the name of Dorothy Langton, left the stage on getting married; she was always called 'Dumps' by her friends.

The success of *The Arcadians* and other shows enabled Howard Talbot to buy a charming country house at Chalfont St Giles called 'Five Diamonds'. If the composer happened to notice a lean and hungry young actor in one of his pieces he would tell him about a wonderful pub down at Chalfont called 'The Five Diamonds' where you could get a cheap meal and also a game of tennis or croquet. Quite a number of actors accepted his invitation to come down to 'the pub' on a Saturday night – in fact 'Dumps' never knew how many would turn up for Sunday lunch. Whenever she protested to Talbot about chucking around too many invitations, he said: 'The poor chap looked as if he could do with a good meal and he'd *never* come if I told him it was my house!'

There was an important difference between Howard Talbot and Lionel Monckton when it came to the business of composing a score. Monckton only wrote at the piano, then got somebody else to orchestrate his numbers. But Howard Talbot, a first rate musician, wrote at a table for the full orchestra, only using his piano when he wanted to hear what a chord sounded like, or if he wanted to play a number over to 'Dumps' when he had a rush job to finish. Whenever Talbot collaborated with Lionel Monckton, he did all the orchestrations.

They collaborated again on the score of *The Mousmé,* the book of which was by Robert Courtneidge and A.M. Thompson. Presented at the Shaftesbury on September 9, 1911, the piece was a melodrama in a Japanese setting, played out by a collection of cardboard characters. The *Daily News* said: 'The authors dare you to take their characters seriously, and that I found impossible . . . Neither Mr Lionel Monckton nor Mr Howard Talbot has written very striking music.' Dan Rolyat (the comedian from *The Arcadians*) tried to raise laughs from threadbare material and couldn't manage it. The characters were all Japanese, and their various shades of broken English helped to make the piece sound even more artificial. The only thing that really moved the bored first night audience was the brilliant staging of an earthquake. *The Mousmé* only ran for 200 performances, and Robert Courtneidge lost heavily on the production.

Paul Rubens, who collaborated at times with Howard Talbot, Lionel Monckton and Sidney Jones, began composing for the stage when he was up at Oxford. This prolific composer wrote either on his own or in collaboration the scores of twenty musical plays in the course of twenty years. Sometimes he wrote his own lyrics and sometimes he also worked on the book. Dark and handsome, Rubens' charming personality made him very popular both in the theatre world and in society. Like Monckton, he had read Law at Oxford, and had acted in undergraduate shows and composed songs for them. He loved acting and once claimed that in *The Knights* by Aristophanes he had memorized 200 lines of Greek verse.

His professional career began when he wrote two numbers for Ellaline Terriss – 'The Little Chinchilla' and 'The China Egg' – which she sang when she took over from Ada Reeve in *The Shop Girl.* George and Weedon Grossmith produced his operetta, *Young Mr Yarde*, at the Royalty in 1898 just as Ada Reeve was making a hit

36. Paul Rubens, a prolific composer, of whom it was said 'he can write a number while you take off your hat and coat'.

with his number, 'Trixie of Upper Tooting' in 'Little Miss Nobody'. Rubens then wrote several songs for Ada Reeve; she sang three of them in *Florodora*, including 'Tact'. He had fallen in love with Ada Reeve and proposed to her during the run of *Florodora*. Ada Reeve was older than Rubens and had been divorced after an unhappy marriage. Though very fond of him, she didn't take him seriously and turned him down.

George Edwardes, always on the look-out for talent, signed up Paul Rubens on the strength of his *Florodora* numbers, and Rubens

PLAY PICTORIAL

37. Isabel Jay as the captivating Sally Hook and G.P. Huntley as her lovable old
father in *Miss Hook of Holland*, a big success composed by Paul Rubens (Prince
of Wales's, 1907).

contributed additional numbers to several shows at the Gaiety and
Daly's. *Three Little Maids*, his first solo score, opened at the Apollo
on May 10, 1902 and ran for over 300 performances. The *Era* said:
'Few men have made such rapid progress in a profession as Paul
Rubens in the one which he has chosen . . .' Rubens also wrote serious
ballads and composed the incidental music for Herbert Beerbohm

192

Tree's production of *Twelfth Night*. Rubens was very delicate, having suffered from a lung disease ever since he was twenty. He might possibly have been cured if he had gone to live in the country where there was better air than in London, but he adored working in the theatre and had no intention of giving up his London life. In between his bad bouts, Rubens had tremendous bursts of activity; most of the time he worked on musical plays for George Edwardes or Robert Courtneidge.

Paul Rubens loved going to parties in town, and sometimes made an appointment to meet Robert Courtneidge at his rooms at midnight to discuss new numbers for a show. Rubens would come in late and start talking to Courtneidge about the new songs with such vivacity that it sounded as if he had only just started the day. The slightest suggestion from Courtneidge would be quite enough to start his agile brain working; soon Rubens would sit down at the piano, smoking a cigarette and polishing his new number, looking as if he hadn't the slightest intention of ever going to bed.

Rubens wrote the music and lyrics of *Miss Hook of Holland*, which Frank Curzon produced at the Prince of Wales's on January 31, 1907; Rubens had also collaborated on the book. G.P. Huntley had a fine part as Mr Hook, an eccentric, lovable old Dutchman in the distillery trade. Isabel Jay played his clever daughter, Miss Hook, and had some excellent numbers, including the bewitching 'Little Miss Wooden Shoes', 'Fly Away, Kite' and a charming bacarolle, 'By the side of the sleeping canal'. 'A Little Pink Petty from Peter', sung by Gracie Leigh as the Hooks' sexy maid, was the hit of the show:

> I've a little pink petty from Peter
> And a little pink petty from John,
> And I've one green and yellow
> From some other fellow,
> And one that I haven't got on.
> I've one made of lovely red flannel
> That came from an Amsterdam store –
> But the point that I'm at,
> Is that *underneath* that –
> Well, I haven't got on any more!

Sometimes Paul Rubens had to miss going to rehearsals of his pieces because he was laid up in bed. He once said: 'Perhaps to be ill and have rehearsals of one's own play going on at the same time is one of the most tantalising things that one could imagine. One has so much time to think of things one would like to do or suggest at rehearsals.'

Paul Rubens and Phyllis Dare met through mutual friends in the theatre. The attractive composer and the exceedingly pretty actress fell madly in love and got engaged; but Rubens felt it would be unfair to marry her unless he could be certain of being cured of consumption. He might have had a chance of a cure, but he wouldn't cut down on his work and refused to live in the country. When his health deteriorated their engagement was broken off by mutual consent, but it made no difference to their love affair. They spent as much time together as possible and when Phyllis Dare went on tour in a musical play, he often travelled up and down the country just to be near her.

Paul Rubens was almost the double of King Alfonso of Spain, which proved embarrassing when he took a holiday in the Balkans to get some local colour for *The Balkan Princess,* when he was writing the score. As he changed trains at Belgrade he was mistaken for King Alfonso. Luckily, the Spanish king was very popular in that part of the world, and a large crowd cheered him heartily as his train steamed out of the station.

The Balkan Princess, presented by Frank Curzon at the Prince of Wales's on February 20, 1910, had music by Paul Rubens, who also wrote the lyrics with Arthur Wimperis; the book was by Frederick Lonsdale and Frank Curzon. *The Balkan Princess* got excellent notices; the *Daily News* said, 'the "straight" story and the pretty thread of sentiment running through it captivated Saturday's audience... Never before has this composer [Paul Rubens] revealed himself in livelier mood... if he does not escape the charge of being a thought reminiscent, his tunes trip along gently on that account'.

The Ruritanian Princess Stephanie has to get married for the sake of her country. In disguise, she tracks down her reluctant suitor, Grand Duke Sergius, at his Bohemian haunt and they fall in love. But Sergius spoils it all by drinking a toast to the downfall of Princess

38. Phyllis Dare introduces the tango to London, partnered by George Grossmith, Jr. in *The Sunshine Girl* at the Gaiety in 1912.

Stephanie! She arrests him on the spot and has him imprisoned in her palace. But his charm works wonders and they are re-united in the end. Isabel Jay and Bertram Wallis had splendid notices for their performances in the main roles. Among the best numbers were 'Love and Laughter', 'Wonderful World' and the burglary duet; but despite good notices, *The Balkan Princess* had rather a short run.

When George Edwardes withdrew *Peggy* from the Gaiety, he commissioned Paul Rubens to write a piece for Phyllis Dare. Besides composing the score of *The Sunshine Girl,* Paul Rubens collaborated on the 'book' and the lyrics. Presented at the Gaiety on February 24, 1912, it told the story of Delia, a nice girl who works in the perfume department of Port Sunshine – a copy of Port Sunlight, Lever's huge model soap factory. Delia has no idea that her fiancé and fellow worker has just inherited the factory. To make sure that she really loves him for himself, he hands over the factory to an aristocratic friend (George Grossmith) who makes a hash of everything, aided and abetted by a petty crook (Teddy Payne). The crook's wife (Connie Ediss) catches up with him before the happy ending.

The Sunshine Girl had an excellent run of 336 performances. The role of Delia suited Phyllis Dare admirably, George Grossmith and Teddy Payne were in fine form, and Connie Ediss brought the house down with her numbers, 'I've been to the Durbar' and 'Take me on the boat to Brighton'. Paul Rubens wrote a sentimental song with a beautiful melody which became very popular and was a standard number for years:

I love the moon, I love the sun,
I love the wild birds, the dawn and the dew,
I love the forest, the flowers and the fun,
But best of all I love you, I love you!

Rubens had written 'I love the moon' when *The Sunshine Girl* was being tried out at Brighton. He was ill at the time, but managed to get up from his bed and call at the stage door with the music. He told the stage door keeper to be sure to hand it to 'Miss Phyllis Dare'; inside he enclosed a note dedicating his song to her.

Three outstanding librettists of the period which ended in the First World War were James Tanner, Owen Hall and Frederick

Lonsdale. James Tanner wrote the books of nearly a score of musical comedies at the Gaiety, and was also the librettist of *The Quaker Girl, A Country Girl* and *The Cingalee,* all produced by George Edwardes. Tanner was tall and very dark – so dark that he was sometimes mistaken for a gipsy. His first job had been as a baggage man in a shipping office. Being stage-struck, he joined Alice Lingarde's Shakesperean company in the 'eighties, playing small parts and asisting with the stage management. After working for Lingarde and Van Biene's comic opera companies, he wrote *The Broken Melody* in 1892, which featured August Van Biene playing the cello.

Van Biene introduced him to George Edwardes, who made him stage manager at the Gaiety. One day Edwardes summoned Tanner and asked him if he could outline a piece that was a cross between French burlesque and Gilbert and Sullivan. Tanner gave him a rough outline of *In Town* the same afternoon, and Edwardes accepted it in the evening. Tanner and Adrian Ross wrote in the dialogue and the 'gags' in a few days – and that was how the first successful musical comedy came into being.

James Tanner had been a jack-of-all-trades before he found his feet in the theatre. He had been so destitute at one time that he couldn't afford the price of a bed and had to sleep out on the Embankment. He told Jimmy Jupp, the Gaiety stage door keeper, that he got the idea for his first play as a result of his talks with a down-and-out on the Embankment. Tanner never forgot the days when he had been so poor that he couldn't even buy himself a cup of coffee. After he had made a corner in Gaiety musical comedies, Tanner became well off, but for years he used to walk down to the Embankment some nights and hand out cash to any of his old mates who were still sleeping out. In the 1900s Tanner began to suffer from cancer and spent most of his time at his home at Gravesend and very seldom came to London. After a long and painful illness he died in a nursing home on June 18, 1915, at the age of fifty six.

Readers may recall that Owen Hall was a nom-de-plume for Jimmy Davis, the journalist who became one of the most popular librettists of his time. An Irish Jew born in Dublin, he started as a solicitor but,

197

after toiling away at the Law for twelve years, he gave it up for journalism. When he wrote *A Gaiety Girl* for George Edwardes, Jimmy Davis was drama critic of *The Sporting Life,* otherwise known as *The Pink 'Un.* Before that he had edited *The Bat,* a provocative weekly paper which, like *Private Eye,* made acid comments on prominent people and sometimes went too far and got sued for libel. Davis never pulled his punches and within a year his libel cases sent the paper bankrupt.

In the 'nineties, his three operettas for Daly's and *Florodora* brought prosperity to Jimmy Davis. He bought an elegant house in Curzon Street where he gave delightful supper parties on Saturdays for his friends in all walks of life, but principally in the theatre. It became a leading centre of 'clean-shirted Bohemians'; a lawyer or a peer might find himself placed next to an opera singer or a music hall star. Sometimes Signor Tosti would sit down at the piano in the first-floor drawing room and improvise wonderful melodies in the early hours of a Sunday morning. And if a new song had been written for a musical play it was sure to be heard first at Curzon Street with the composer at the piano.

Of medium height, Jimmy Davis had a small moustache and a sharp pair of eyes. A witty man, he could be very malicious at times, and make enemies for himself. He was addicted to backing horses and, as the majority of them lost, it was a very expensive pastime. After George Edwardes had paid him £2,000 for the libretto of *A Greek Slave,* Davis went racing and lost every penny in the course of three weeks. He had married a Miss Andrade and had several children, but she found it impossible to cope with the ups and downs of Jimmy Davis.

After writing *Florodora* in 1899, Davis (or Owen Hall) had no comparable success with his pieces. In 1905 he landed himself in debt, on top of which he had to settle some costly libel actions; then for several months he suffered from acute gastritis. Jimmy Davis died on April 9, 1907 in relative obscurity and left hardly any money for his family. It was a wretched ending for the man who had given London playgoers four of the most entertaining musical plays of the era.

Frederick Lonsdale, who became world famous for his comedies in the 'twenties, began his theatrical career as a librettist. When he wrote *The King of Cadonia* in 1908 the critics praised him for his gift of writing clever dialogue and his knack of making royal personages convincing on the stage. Yet Freddy Lonsdale, the son of a Jersey tobacconist, had never met a king or queen in his life then; he had knocked about the world as a private in the Army and been a rolling stone. He always used to boast, 'Thank God I'm not a gentleman!'

He eloped with his wife, Lesley, when he was penniless. But she had faith in his talent during all the setbacks of their early married life and was indirectly responsible for his introduction to Frank Curzon, the manager who presented, *The King of Cadonia*. Curzon also produced *The Balkan Princess,* of which Lonsdale was part author, in 1910. Freddy Lonsdale was broke again two years later when George Edwardes asked him to call at Daly's. Edwardes was still the leading impresario of musical plays, and this seemed a great opportunity. Edwardes and Robert Evett, his new partner, wanted to get a Continental piece adapted into English and had reached an impasse. Edwardes handed Lonsdale the script and a cheque for £100, and asked him to read it at once and come back later and give them his comments.

Lonsdale returned to Daly's in the afternoon, put the script on George Edwardes's desk, and slowly tore the cheque into pieces. Edwardes, astonished, asked why he had done it. 'Because no man living could do anything with this story', replied Lonsdale. It turned out that he was right. The Guv'nor shelved the story and revived his old success, *A Country Girl.* But he needed a new piece to follow it and told Robert Evett, 'Send for the young man who tore up the cheque.'

Edwardes put Freddy Lonsdale under contract to write libretti for Daly's, which was the beginning of Lonsdale's remarkable run of successes. In 1915 he wrote *Betty* for Daly's with a score by Paul Rubens, which had a long run. And in 1917 he wrote the 'book' of *The Maid of the Mountains* to the score of Fraser-Simson. It starred José Collins, and ran through the rest of the war for a total of 1,352 performances.

It is time to return to the Edwardian composers. In my opinion the ones who came closest to Sullivan's light music were Sir Edward German, Sidney Jones and Lionel Monckton. It was their misfortune that no librettist could compare with Sullivan's great collaborator, W.S. Gilbert, consequently none of their scores are equal to *The Mikado* or *Patience* or *The Gondoliers* or *Iolanthe,* to name only four of the Savoy operas.

After 1911 there was a fundamental change in light music when ragtime and jazz invaded England from America, and waltzes and polkas and romantic ballads became relics of the past. Even the Gilbert and Sullivan operas went out of fashion after their great days, and had to wait till the 'twenties for their revival. 'Alexander's Ragtime Band' by Irving Berlin conquered the world in the same way that Johann Strauss had once swept the board with his waltzes from Vienna. In London the public flocked to the Hippodrome to see the Americanized revues of Albert de Courville with titles like 'Hullo, Ragtime', 'Hullo, Tango!' and 'Razzle-Dazzle', and things were never the same again.

This survey has concentrated on the outstanding English operettas of a period ending in 1914, the year which was to change the face of Europe. In the Epilogue I shall briefly trace the careers of the Edwardian composers, lyrists and librettists from the time of the First World War.

EPILOGUE

FORTUNES OF WAR

On New Year's Day, 1914, very few people expected that England, France and Russia would be fighting the First World War against Germany and her Allies in the summer. When an unhinged youth shot the Archduke Ferdinand at Sarajevo, it seemed a minor affair; the war only broke out because Germany under the Kaiser had determined to go to war with Russia and seized the Archduke's assassination as a pretext. When England declared war against Germany on August 4 it brought to an end the leisurely Edwardian age that had spilled over into the new reign of George V.

On August 4 George Edwardes had the misfortune to be at Bad Nauheim, a German health spa, having gone there in the hope of finding a cure for his serious heart condition. He was overweight and had already had a stroke, and for the past two years his three theatres had been losing money while he was hors de combat. The Germans interned Edwardes at Bad Nauheim, only allowing him to go within one mile of his hotel, the worst medicine they could have given this extrovert Irishman. After his second stroke in 1915, the German authorities allowed him to travel home. But he returned to England a broken man and died on October 4, leaving his theatrical affairs in a bad state. What a sad exit for the Guv'nor who had dominated the musical plays of London for two decades!

Paul Rubens was still in his thirties when England went to war, but his lung disease had never been cured. Although he couldn't do any war work, he 'did his bit' by writing musical plays which entertained the troops on leave and kept up their morale, and in 1916 composed one of the best known recruiting songs of the war:

> We don't want to lose you,
> But we think you ought to go,
> For your King and your country
> Both need you so.

The war made no difference to his romance with Phyllis Dare, who sang 'We don't want to lose you' in a revue at the Palace and got encored every night. Rubens had no difficulty in adapting his music to the new jazz rhythms; working in feverish bursts of activity he composed the scores of *Betty* (Daly's) and *To-Night's the Night* (The Gaiety) in 1915, both of which were immensely popular. The following year he collaborated with Sidney Jones on the score of *The Happy Day*.

But Rubens had put all his remaining strength into his compositions. At the beginning of 1917 he was suddenly taken ill and died on February 5. Phyllis Dare was heartbroken and, although she outlived him by fifty years, she never really recovered from the tragedy of his death. Everyone in the theatre mourned Paul Rubens. Ellaline Terriss described him aptly as 'one of the most popular men who has ever written for the light musical theatre' and William Boosey paid him this tribute – 'He was generosity itself, and charming to all the world – a gentleman in the truest and most delicate sense of the word.'

Ivan Caryll had the most enjoyable war of all the composers, living in the lap of luxury in the United States three thousand miles away from Flanders. When war broke out he was well established as a top flight Broadway composer of musical plays. He had sailed off to America four years earlier, partly because he was jealous of Lionel Monckton for always writing the hit songs in their musical comedies. He had written *The Little Café* and *Oh, Oh Delphine* for Broadway and sometimes collaborated on shows with the celebrated British team of P.G. Wodehouse and Guy Bolton. Everyone called him Felix – since Felix Tilkins was his real name – but Wodehouse nicknamed him Fabulous Felix for good reasons.

Fabulous Felix had become more of a peacock than ever; he had main residences on Long Island and in Paris, also a villa at Deauville overlooking the racecourse. His second wife was Maud Hill, the Gaiety actress, and they had five children; in the villa at Deauville he had five bathrooms for his five offspring. He handled Broadway theatre managers with great skill, taking a suite at the Knickerbocker Hotel, New York, then inviting them to visit him there and make an offer for his latest piece.

His beard had grown enormous and Wodehouse believed it was a great asset to him. He generally suggested a French piece to managers, assuring them that the French author was an impossible man to haggle with and demanded royalties twice as high as the going rate. The Broadway managers fell for this story and paid Fabulous Felix double royalties on behalf of the absent French author (although the latter had already sold his rights to Felix for a few francs). Wodehouse swore that the managers were all hypnotized by the composer's magnificent beard.

Ivan Caryll returned to England soon after the Armistice for the production of *The Kiss Call,* a musical comedy which only did moderately well. But in 1919 George Grossmith opened the Winter Garden Theatre with Caryll's operetta, *Kissing Time,* a tremendous success with Leslie Henson, George Grossmith, Phyllis Dare and Yvonne Arnaud in the principal roles. Caryll still thought money existed only for the purpose of entertaining himself and his friends. The composer was back in the States, in the middle of rehearsals for his new Broadway show, when he suddenly fell ill and died from cancer on November 29, 1921. Owing to his crazy extravagance his family were left badly off.

During the war Lionel Monckton collaborated again with Howard Talbot on the score of *The Boy,* a musical farce adapted from Pinero's play, *The Magistrate.* Opening at the Adelphi on September 15, 1917, with W.H. Berry as the erring magistrate, it ran for 800 performances. Monckton's marriage to Gertie Millar had broken up before the war, but they had arranged an amicable separation. Marriage to Gertie Millar, an idol of the Edwardian theatre, had proved too much for a retiring personality like Monckton. No matter how busy Gertie Millar might be on the stage, she found time to encourage her admirers from the Duke of Westminster to business magnates. Monckton found it impossible to compose music and keep up with her circle of friends and admirers. He seemed happy to return to his bachelor existence, spending a lot of time at first nights and with kindred spirits at the Green Room Club. He loved strumming away at the piano in the card room till the early hours of the morning.

When *The Boy* came off in 1919 his niece, Mrs Dorothy Miskin, asked Monckton what he was going to write next. He replied, 'Nothing! I'm not going to bother to write any more music for other men to mess about!' An Edwardian in spirit, he was nearly sixty and felt out of sympathy with the new jazz music that was all the rage. Thanks to his many hit songs he could afford to retire in the 'twenties. He began to suffer from bronchitis, but still went to first nights; sometimes he went alone, looking rather a pathetic figure. After first nights he looked in at the Green Room and regaled the members with his opinion of the new piece.

In 1922 Monckton had to leave his house in Russell Square because the lease had run out. But he was so devoted to his family of dogs and cats that he bought another big house in Gordon Square, telling his relations: 'I have to find a square so that the dogs can leave their visiting cards and the cats can join their choral society.' He died suddenly on February 15, 1924.

Howard Talbot was the unluckiest of the Edwardian composers: on the advice of one of the Rothschilds he put all his savings into Russian oil shares, but when the Bolsheviks took over Russia in 1917 his shares became worthless. The debacle didn't worry him at first because his music for *The Boy* was earning him a good income. After it came off, he collaborated with the young Ivor Novello on the score of *Who's Hooper?*. Produced at the Adelphi and starring W.H. Berry, it had a long run.

Howard and 'Dumps' Talbot were very happily married and blessed with four daughters. But in the early 'twenties his health broke down and suddenly put an end to his career as a composer. He had contracted a lung disease, probably caused by the dust from the powdered resin of a violin in one of the orchestras he was conducting for George Edwardes. Howard and 'Dumps' Talbot took a big farm at Bletchingley and left an unscrupulous man in charge of it. He swindled them of every penny and, although the Talbots prosecuted him, they got nothing back. With very little money coming in from his music, Talbot rented a self-contained flat in Reigate. He was a great joker and, although his health steadily deteriorated, he never complained and would only retire to bed if the doctor ordered it.

By the mid-twenties he regularly had bad nights and woke up feeling very breathless. His daughter Joy had to help him to get dressed, then he would sit in his chair composing at a table while the two youngest daughters played games around his feet. If it was a fine day a man would call for him and push him off in a Bath chair for his 'constitutional'. He would rest in the afternoon and then play card games with the children. After the young ones had gone to bed he would play a game of Chess with Joy Talbot, or play Bridge with 'Dumps' and others. They were still living at Reigate when he died on September 12, 1928.

At one time there had been a project for Howard Talbot to collaborate with Ian Hay on a musical play, but it fell through because he was too ill to undertake the score. Ian Hay wrote this letter to 'Dumps' Talbot after his death:

21, Bruton St.,
  Berkeley Square, W.   14/9/28

Dear Mrs. Talbot,

I am deeply grieved to hear of your husband's death yesterday. The last time I saw him I was genuinely shocked at his appearance, for he was obviously seriously ill; but I hoped that with his wonderful courage and strength of character he would pull round in time. However, it was not to be, and in consequence we have all to mourn the loss of a brilliant musician and a most remarkable man... I would just like to say how proud I was to have known him, and how sorry I am that I had not the honour of appearing as his collaborator.

Ian Hay Beith.[1]

Howard Talbot left under £400. 'Dumps' coped with the financial crisis by enrolling with N.O.D.A. as a producer of musical plays, which meant she had to travel around the country a good deal. While she was away her eldest daughter, Betty, acted as a second mother to the young girls and Joy went out to work and only came home at week ends. It was sad that Talbot's family should have been left in such straits all because he had put his money into Russian oil shares.

When war broke out, Adrian Ross, the scholarly lyric writer, joined the Artists' Rifles. Being bronchial and rather overweight, he proved unfit for service and was invalided out of the Army in 1915. During the rest of the war he was very busy working on musical plays; he wrote the lyrics of *Betty* and contributed lyrics to *The Boy* and to *Arlette.* He continued working on shows after the war. In 1919 he wrote the lyrics of the comic opera, *Monsieur Beaucaire,* which had a delightful score by André Messager, and the following year wrote the lyrics of *A Southern Maid* for José Collins at Daly's.

In 1922 Ross was commissioned to write the 'book' and lyrics of *Lilac Time,* a romantic version of Schubert's life with songs by the German composer. He was not very well off at the time, and all the family kept their fingers crossed hoping for a success. *Lilac Time* opened in December and did badly in the first few weeks. But in the New Year business suddenly picked up, and the Schubert operetta became one of the greatest money-spinners of the decade and ran for 628 performances. Adrian Ross wrote little for the theatre in his last years and died in 1933, aged 74.

The war made a vital difference to the career of Percy Greenbank, another outstanding lyrist. When George Edwardes died in 1915 the bottom dropped out of his world. Greenbank needed the incentive of having to work to a deadline; without the Guv'nor he had

[1]Howard Talbot papers.

no more deadlines to meet. No other musical play producer gave him a long term contract as Edwardes had done, yet Greenbank refused to push himself when he needed work on a show. He never employed an agent and was inclined to wait for a West End producer to get in touch and commission him to write lyrics. However, during the war he contributed lyrics to *The Boy, To-night's the night* and *Tina*.

Paul Rubens had collaborated with Haydn Wood on the score of *Tina*. Percy Greenbank came home after a late night rehearsal and wrote an extra number in the early hours of the morning. He had to interrupt the family holiday by going into the village post office at Roydon, Essex, and dictating his lyric to Paul Rubens into the open phone. People in the post office at Roydon were quite shocked as they heard Greenbank dictating the slightly suggestive lyric of a number entitled 'Please don't Flirt with Me.'

In 1915 he moved out of London with the family and rented a house at Chalfont St Giles, very near his great friend, Howard Talbot, who was then at 'Five Diamonds'. In 1922, Greenbank rented 'Meadowside', a new house at Rickmansworth with an acre and a half of ground with only three trees in it. Greenbank was delighted with the chance of indulging his passion for gardening to the full; he had green fingers and, starting from scratch, made a splendid garden at Meadowside.

Percy Greenbank, Lionel Monckton and Howard Talbot were founder members of the Performing Right Society, which managed to negotiate a special deal for stage composers and lyric writers on their 'small performing rights'. When Greenbank wrote the lyrics of *The Street Singer,* produced at the Lyric in June, 1924, he received royalties for the first time; the piece ran for 360 performances and earned him a bigger income than he had ever had in his life. In 1926 he adapted *Yvonne* from the French and also wrote the lyrics.

In 1932 he decided to leave 'Meadowside' and take a flat in London. He had been so carried away with the garden that he had been neglecting his lyrics. 'I've *got* to get out and sit in a flat and pull the blinds down', he told his wife. During the following years Greenbank kept fairly busy, writing lyrics and sometimes writing for *Punch*. He eased off in his seventies, but for many years he served on the board of the Performing Right Society. He died at the ripe old age of ninety on December 8, 1968; his only regret had been missing the celebration of his Diamond Wedding in 1962 owing to his wife's death three months earlier.

Sidney Jones made little headway in his career during the war. After collaborating with Paul Rubens on *The Girl from Utah* in 1913, they collaborated again on the score of *The Happy Day* in 1916. Jones only composed nine of the numbers and was astonished at the speed at which Rubens worked; he told his wife, 'Paul Rubens can write a number while you take off your hat and coat.' His two sons came home on leave from the Army and went to see *The Happy Day*. Arthur Jones came home whistling 'The Boys are Marching', a stirring number composed by Paul Rubens. Jones was quite upset because his son had not picked one of his own compositions. Although Sidney Jones was only fifty at the end of the war, he had already begun to fade into the shadows as an operetta composer. He failed to adapt his music to the jazz-mad 'twenties and couldn't break away from the Edwardian tradition when waltzes dominated the stage and the heroine was wooed to the strains of a sentimental ballad.

After the war Jones wrote several operettas in the Edwardian tradition, but none of them got produced. For a time he lived in hopes that his piece, *The Little Milliner,* with lyrics by Adrian Ross, would obtain a London production, but it never materialized. *The Geisha* had been revived in 1908 with little success; it had a second limited revival in 1930 and never appeared afterwards in the West End. However, *The Geisha* and *San Toy* were tremendously popular with amateur societies and brought him in quite a substantial income. Sidney Jones died in London at the age of seventy-seven on January 29, 1946. It is a reflection of the public's taste that the younger generation had scarcely ever heard of him, and Jones has never been given full credit for his achievements before the First World War.

When the war broke out, Edward German was still living on his own in Hall Road and composing very little music. In 1913 he had narrowly escaped being killed in an accident when his taxi collided with a bus in the Edgware Road; the shock had left him with a permanent physical weakness. German felt completely out of touch with the modern music of Stravinsky and others, and loathed Americanized musical shows with strident jazz numbers. He wrote to a friend: 'I waste quires of paper on sketches and ideas which I do not feel worth developing. I fancy the root of it all is the ultra-modern school of composition; it is a language which E.G. will never acquire.'

During the war he set to music Rudyard Kipling's topical poem, 'Have you any news of my boy Jack?, which became very popular after Dame Clara Butt had sung it at a Royal Philharmonic Concert.

After the war German conducted his works at a number of music festivals and concerts all over England; his comic operas, *Merrie England* and *Tom Jones,* and his incidental music for Shakespeare's plays were always great favourites. He was forced to realize in 1927 that conducting was straining his eyes and taxing his remaining strength. When his eyesight began to fail he had an operation, which eventually resulted in him losing the sight of one eye. His great friend, Sir Alexander Mackenzie, wrote to him:

15, Regents Park Road, N.W.
Nov. 16, 1927.

My dear Edward,

I may not begin to say how terribly sorry I am to have your news – besides you know how all our sympathies go out to you. The enforced rest and quiet will do you good in other directions, but are damned hard to carry out! Meanwhile, be a good boy and do as you are bidden. And, above all, stay *cheerio* like your own happy music.

Of course 'ACMs' must know about your temporary trouble – but they are discreet fellows – except perhaps in the matter of Burgundy – and will do their best to enliven you.

No more at present, from your old friend,

A.C. Mackenzie.[1]

---

[1] Letter in the possession of Mrs Winifred German.

The ACMs mentioned by Mackenzie referred to a little club which took its name from his initials; its four members dined with friends on their birthdays and other special occasions, generally at the Café Royal. The members were Sir Alexander Mackenzie, Edward German, Herman Finck, the composer and conductor, and Colonel Mackenzie Rogan, Director of Music of the Goldstream Guards. When German was on the brink of sixty-six, he was knighted for his services to music on February 16, 1928 – an honour that was greatly overdue in the opinion of the British musical world. German had retained his great interest in cricket. When Herman Finck asked him why he had only lived half a life by never getting married, German remarked drily, 'Women do not understand cricket.'

Another of German's close friends was Sir Edward Elgar, the leading British composer. After German wrote to congratulate him on his seventieth birthday, Elgar replied charmingly, 'My music cannot give you one hundredth of the pleasure I have had from your music.' *Merrie England* and *Tom Jones* were never revived in London after their original productions in 1902 and 1907 respectively. The musical critics consider that German's music has stood up remarkably well to the test of time, but that the weakness lies in the libretti, a view which I certainly share. William Boosey, in his book of memoirs, says, 'There is no doubt that Edward German's delightful scores, *Merrie England* and *Tom Jones,* would have permanently held the stage if the librettos had been equal to the music.' Edward German died peacefully on November 11, 1936.

Leslie Stuart, once the most popular song writer in England, went bankrupt a year before the war broke out. But Stuart, a resilient character, refused to accept defeat and went on the halls in 1915, playing a selection of his famous songs like 'Lily of Laguna', 'Little Dolly Daydreams' and 'Soldiers of the Queen', which were sung by his brother, Lester Barrett. There had been an unsophisticated strain of elementary jazz in his last Edwardian pieces, but Stuart stopped composing operettas after *Peggy* in 1911. In 1921 he undertook a strenuous tour of the United States where his music had always been very popular; he toured America from coast to coast and had a spectacular success.

But when he returned to England none of the music hall circuits would book him; he was regarded as a has-been, and no theatre management was prepared to commission him to write a score. However, when *Palladium Pleasures* opened on February 24, 1926, fortune smiled on Stuart once again. Vivian Ellis had composed the score and its stars included Billy Merson, Lorna and Toots Pounds, Norah Bayes, the American singer, and Anton Dolin. The final item was 'Leslie Stuart's Dream Songs'. The curtain rose on an elderly, silver-haired man with a sad expression seated at a piano; then Leslie Stuart began to play softly.

W. Macqueen Pope, who was at the first night, wrote:

The audience stilled and listened. From his skilful fingers, ranging over the keys, came the strains of the songs he had given to the world, songs that the audience had known and remembered since childhood.

Many of them had never seen him before, but they knew his songs. He wove a spell around them and that great audience began to nod and move in time to the music. And then – it began to sing.

Stuart played a few introductory chords afterwards, then the orchestra took up the music of a song that swelled up into 'Soldiers of the Queen'. The curtains parted to reveal the stage packed with the entire company dressed as soldiers, and accompanied by the Metropolitan Brass Band and the Caledonian Pipe Band. This stirring finale made a great impression on the first night audience of *Palladium Pleasures,* and never failed to move the audience during its long run.

Leslie Stuart had finally managed to make his English comeback. He was given a big contract to tour the halls with his best known numbers, which his daughter, May, sang to his piano accompaniment. Stuart got a marvellous reception wherever he appeared, and audiences revelled in these nostalgic old songs. His triumph gave him fresh confidence and he composed a new operetta entitled *Nina*. A management agreed to produce it and set a date for the first rehearsal. But before then Leslie Stuart had a heart attack and died a few days later at his daughter May's house at Richmond on March 27, 1928.

One can safely claim that Leslie Stuart lives on with such songs as 'Lily of Laguna' and 'Soldiers of the Queen'. This was recognized by the city of Manchester just before the Second World War when the civic authorities put up a bust of him in the Public Library – although the composer was actually born in Southport – with a plaque underneath it saying:

Leslie Stuart – 1866–1928

A son of Lancashire and composer of 'Lily of Laguna' etc. His music moved millions to song.

It is quite possible that more numbers by Leslie Stuart are remembered today than those of any of the other light composers who followed Arthur Sullivan. Or perhaps the distinction may belong to Edward German or Lionel Monckton. This is really an academic question which the most advanced computer would be hard pressed to answer. When one has studied English operettas up till the First World War period, there is only one positive fact to be stated: Gilbert and Sullivan, or Sullivan and Gilbert, are the supreme masters of English operetta.

When the lights go dim in a theatre anywhere in the English speaking world, and the orchestra finishes playing that overture with a familiar Japanese style in the music, and the curtain goes up on the town of Tipitu and the chorus of Oriental noblemen are discovered standing and sitting in attitudes – then *The Mikado* is being played for something like the millionth time; and very few men and women in the audience will be able to resist its enchanting music or sit poker-faced at the humour of the dialogue and the wit of the lyrics.

BIBLIOGRAPHY

Books

Allen, Reginald, *The First Night Gilbert and Sullivan*, Chappell, 1976.

Archer, William, *Real Conversations*, Heinemann, 1904.

Ayre, Leslie, *The Gilbert and Sullivan Companion*, W.H. Allen, 1972.

Baily, Leslie, *The Gilbert and Sullivan Book*, Cassell, 1952.
   Gilbert and Sullivan and their World, Thames and Hudson, 1973.

Bancroft, George, *Stage and Bar*, Faber, 1939.

Barrington, Rutland, *Rutland Barrington*, Grant Richards, 1928.

Bolitho, Hector, *Marie Tempest*, Cobden Sanderson, 1936.

Bond, Jessie, *Life and Reminiscences of Jessie Bond*, John Lane, 1930.

Boosey, William, *Fifty Years of Music*, Ernest Benn, 1931.

Booth, J.B., *London Town*, Werner Laurie, 1929.

Cellier, Francois and Bridgeman, Cunningham, *Gilbert and Sullivan and D'Oyly Carte*, Sir Isaac Pitman and Son, 1914.

Coffin, Hayden, *Hayden Coffin's Book*, Alston Rivers, 1930.

Courtneidge, Robert, *I Was an Actor Once*, Hutchinson, 1933.

Dark, Sidney and Grey, Rowland, *W.S. Gilbert – His Life and Letters*, Methuen, 1953.

Donaldson, Frances, *Freddy Lonsdale*, Heinemann, 1957.

Dunhill, Thomas, *Sullivan's Comic Operas*, Edward Arnold, 1929.

Finck, Herman, *My Melodious Memories*, Hutchinson, 1937.

Glover, James, *Jimmy Glover – His Book*, Methuen, 1911.

Grossmith, George, *A Society Clown*, Arrowsmith, 1888.

Hicks, Sir Seymour, *Twenty-five Years of an Actor's Life*, Alston Rivers, 1910.

Hollingshead, John, *Gaiety Chronicles*, Constable, 1898.

Hughes, Gervase, *Composers of Operettas*, Macmillan, 1962.

Hyman, Alan, *The Gaiety Years*, Cassell, 1975.

Irving, Lawrence, *Henry Irving*, Faber, 1951.

Jupp, James, *The Gaiety Stage Door*, Cape, 1923.

Lawrence, Arthur, *Sir Arthur Sullivan*, James Bowden, 1899.

Lehmann, R.C., *Memories of Half a Century*, Smith Elder, 1908.

Leslie, Anita, *The Fabulous Mr Jerome*, Hutchinson 1954

Lubbock, Mark, *The Complete Book of Light Opera*, London, 1962.

Lytton, Sir Henry, *Secrets of a Savoyard,* Jarrolds, 1927.

Mander, Raymond and Mitchenson, Joe, *The Lost Theatres of London,* Hart-Davis, 1968.

The Theatres of London, Hart-Davis, 1961.

Pearson, Hesketh, *Gilbert and Sullivan,* Hamish Hamilton, 1935.

Gilbert, His Life and Strife, Methuen, 1957.

Pope, W. Macqueen, *Gaiety, Theatre of Enchantment,* W.H. Allen, 1949.

The Melody Lingers On, W.H. Allen, 1950.

Reeve, Ada, *Take it for a Fact,* Heinemann, 1954.

Scott, Margaret Clement, Mrs, *Old Days in Bohemian London,* London, 1919.

Scott, William Herbert, *Edward German,* Cecil Palmer, 1932.

Stedman, Jane W. *Gilbert before Sullivan,* Routledge and Kegan Paul, 1969.

Sullivan, Herbert and Flower, Newman, *Sir Arthur Sullivan, His Life Letters and Diaries,* Cassell, 1927.

Terriss, Ellaline, *Just a Little Bit of String,* Hutchinson, 1935.

Winslow, D. Forbes, *Daly's,* W.H. Allen, 1944.

Wodehouse, P.G. and Bolton, Guy, *Bring on the Girls,* Herbert Jenkins, 1954.

Wolfson, John, *Final Curtain,* Chappell, 1976.

Young, Percy M., *Sir Arthur Sullivan,* W. Norton and Co., New York, 1971.

Journals

The Daily News.

The Daily Mail.

The Daily Telegraph.

The Evening News.

The Era.

Gilbert and Sullivan Journal, The Official Publication of the Gilbert and Sullivan Society.

The Illustrated London News.

Punch.

The Times.

Who's Who in the Theatre, Editions 1–6, J.M. Pitman.

GILBERT AND SULLIVAN'S COMIC OPERAS

The theatres and years in which they were first presented
in London are given in brackets.

Thespis (Gaiety, 1871) 12-14. First
night: 15-16 18, 19, 21, 36

Trial by Jury (Royalty, Soho, 1875)
20, First night: 21-2, 23-5

The Sorcerer (Opèra Comique, 1877)
25, First night: 26-7, 43, 56,
142, 170

H.M.S. Pinafore (Opèra Comique,
1878) 27-8, First night: 29-30,
31, 35, 37, 41-2, 48, 61, 164

Pirates of Penzance, The (Opèra
Comique, 1880) 11, 35, New
York premiere, Fifth Avenue:
136, 38, 41, 61, 68

Patience (Opèra Comique, 1881)
First night: 44-5, 46.
Transferred to Savoy: 47, 48,
64, 200

Iolanthe (Savoy, 1882) 48-9, First
night: 50-1, 52, 62, 158, 200

Princess Ida (Savoy, 1883) 53, First
night 54-5, 55, 97

Mikado, The (Savoy, 1885) xi, xii,
56-7, First night: 58-9, 60-1, 63-
4, 70, 77, 84, 88, 116, 125, 132,
135, 164, 186, 200, 214

Ruddigore (Savoy, 1887) 10, 11, 70-
1, First night: 77, 78-9, 89, 125

Yeomen of the Guard, The (Savoy,
1888) xi, 81, First night: 82-3,
84-5

Gondoliers, The (Savoy, 1889) xii,
85, First night: 86-7, 88, 90-2,
94, 97, 103, 107, 116, 164, 200

Utopia Limited (Savoy, 1893) First
night: 114-6, 125, 166

Grand Duke, The (Savoy, 1896) 132,
First night: 134-5, 142

INDEX OF OPERETTAS

Incorporating Gaiety burlesques, musical comedies,
revues, operettas, comic operas and operas.

Ages Ago 5, 10-11
Arcadians, The xii, 186-7
Arlette 208
Artist's Model, An 126-30, 132

Balkan Princess, The 194-6
Beauty Stone, The 142
Beggars Opera, The 4
Belle Helène, La 19
Belle of Brittany, The 187
Belle of Mayfair, The 175-6
Belle of New York, The 175
Betty 199, 204, 208
Blue Moon, The 186
Boy, The 205-6, 208
Broken Melody, The 197

Carmen 170
Chinese Honeymoon, A 184-6
Circus Girl, The 119, 140
Cinder Ellen up-too-late 105
Cingalee, The 197
Claude Duval 107
Cloches de Corneville, Les- 19
Contrabandista, La (revived later as
   The Chieftain) 126, 132
Country Girl, A 159, 161-2, 197, 199
Cox and Box 5

Dorothy xii, 67-70, 72-3, 78-81, 103, 126
Duchess of Gantzig, The 120

Earl and the Girl, The 120
Emerald Isle, The 145-7, 151-2, 154, 155

Fallen Fairies 165-8

Fille de Madame Angot, La 19
Florodora xii, 169-70, 172, 174, 191, 198

Geisha, The xii, 135-41, 169, 210
Girl from Utah, The 210
Grand Duchess of Gerolstein, The 19
Greek Slave, A 141-2, 198

Haddon Hall 111, 113
Hallo, Ragtime 200
Hallo, Tango 200
Happy Arcadia 12
Happy Day, The 204, 210
Happy Hampstead 19
Havana 176-7

In Town 105-6, 114, 197
Ivanhoe 90-1, 98-102, 107

Joan of Arc 123

King of Cadonia, The 177-8, 199
Kiss Call, The 205
Kissing Time 205

Lilac Time 208
Little Café, The 204
Little Cherub, The 120
Little Jack Shepherd 65-7
Little Milliner, The 210
Little Miss Nobody 191

Maid of the Mountains, The 199
Merrie England 155-8, 211-2
Messenger Boy, The 159
Miss Hook of Holland 192-3

Monsieur Beaucaire 208
Monte Carlo 183-4
Monte Cristo junior 72-3
Mousmé, The 190
Mountebanks, The 103-5
Musical Chess Tournament, A 183
My Girl 119
My Lady Molly 177

Nautch Girl, The 107, 116
Nina 212
No Cards 5

Oh Oh Delphine! 204
Orchid, The 159, 161
Our Island Home 11
Our Miss Gibbs 161

Palladium Pleasures 213
Peggy 180, 196, 212
Lérichole, La 19, 20, 22
Petit Faust, Le 19
Pocohontas 107
Princess of Kensington, A 158

Quaker Girl, The 121, 161, 178-80, 197

Razzle Dazzle 200
Red Hussar, The 107
Robert the Devil 13
Rose of Persia, The 143, 145
Runaway Girl, The 119

San Toy 143-5, 159, 161, 186, 210
School Girl, The 175-6
See See 177
Shop Girl, The 116-9, 125, 132, 190
Southern Maid, A 208
Street Singer, The 209

Three Little Maids 192
Tina 209
Tom Jones 163-5, 211-2
Tonight's the Night 204, 208
Toreador, The 158, 159

Vicar of Bray, The 107-8, 111

Wapping Old Stairs 183
Who's Hooper? 206

Young Mr. Yarde 190
Yvonne 209

GENERAL INDEX

A.C.M. Club   212
Aesthetic Movement   43-4
Albert, Prince Consort   7
Alexander, Sir George   154
Alexandra, Princess (later Queen
   Alexandra)   71
Alfonso, King of Spain   194
Anderson, Mary   7
Archer, William   141
Archduke Frederick   203
Aristophanes   190
Arnaud, Yvonne   12
Augarde, Adrienne   128

Bab Ballads   17, 43
Baily, Edward Hodgson ("Watercart
   Baily")   25, 34-5
Bancroft, Sir Squire   17, 64
Barker, Richard   34-5
Barlow, Sir Thomas   146-7
Barnett, Alice   40, 126
Barnett, Clara   7
Barrett, Lester   212
Barrett, Tom see Stuart, Leslie
Barrington Rutland   26-9, 36, 42, 44-5,
   52, 55, 58, 60, 70, 72, 86, 89, 110, 111,
   113, 115, 126, 135, 144, 162
Bat, The   198
Bayes, Norah   213
BBC   187
Bendall, Wilfred   142
Berlin, Irving   200
Bennett, Joseph   71
Berry, W.H.   176-7, 206
Blanche, Ada   188
Blande, Edith   108

Bolton, Guy   204
Bond, Jessie   48, 50, 52, 58, 72, 82, 89, 110,
   126, 134, 185
Boote, Rosie (later Marchioness of
   Headfort)   120
Boosey, William   147, 204, 212
Bottomley, Horatio   172
Boyce, Ethel   153-4
Braham, Harry   108
Braham, Leonora   58, 78
Brandram, Rosina   58, 91, 113, 155
Bridgeman, Cunningham   104
Brunel, Isambard Kingdom   8
Burkem Billie   128
Burnand, Sir Frank C.   4, 5, 43, 125-6, 132
Butt, Dame Clara   211
Byron, H.J.   17

Carr, Osmond   106, 126, 153
Caryll, Ivan (Felix Tilkins)   xii, 114, 117-
   21, 204-5
Cavour restaurant   110
Caste   17
Cecil, Arthur   5, 11
Cellier, Alfred   xii, 36, 61, 67-9, 79-80,
   103, 104
Cellier, Francois   54, 104
Cellier, Peter   xii
Chapel Royal   6, 36, 104
Chappell, music publishers   69, 147
Chappell, Tom   25, 30, 110
Chase, Pauline   128
Churchill, Lord Randolph   123
Clay, Frederick   5, 12, 36, 53
Coffin, Hayden   68-9, 80, 127-8, 130-1,
   135, 140-2, 144, 162-5, 177

Collard, Augustus Drake   25
Collingbourne, Florence   4
Collins, Josè   199, 208
Colonel, The   43-4
Comic Opera Syndicate   25, 27-8, 30, 34
Composers of Operettas   117
Comyns Carr, J   142, 147
Conan Doyle, Sir Arthur   142
Cooper, Hall & Co.   49
Courtneidge, Robert   xiii, 163-4, 189, 193
Courtneidge, Mrs. Robert   189
Creake, Reginald   183-4
Cross, Arthur   183, 189
Cross, Dorothy "Dumps" (Mrs. Howard
      Talbot)   189, 206-8
Curzon, Frank   xiii, 193-4, 199

Dam, H.J.   116
Dance, Sir George   110, 184
Dare, Phyllis   180, 194-6, 204-5
Davies, Ben   70, 79, 101
Davis, Jimmy *see* Hall, Owen
Davis, Mrs. Jimmy   198
Davis, Tom   169
de Courville Albert   200
Denny, W.H. 87
Dickens, Charles   13
Disraeli, Benjamin (later Lord
      Beaconsfield)   29
Divver, Justice   6
Doisy, Arthur   57, 135
Dolaro, Madame Selina,   20, 22
Dolin, Anton   213
D'Oyly Carte, Richard   xi, xiv, 19-22, 25-
      8, 30-2, 34-6, 38, 41-2, 44. *Opens
      Savoy Theatre*   47-9, 54-6, 61, 63-4,
      70-1, 81, 84-5, 88, 90 *Quarrel with
      Gilbert*   92-9, 101-3, 115, 116, 125,
      132, 134-5, 142, 145-7, 151
Drake   168
Duff, American theatre manager   61
Dumas, Alexandre   72
Du Maurier, George   43

Ediss, Connie   175, 196
Edinburgh, Duke of   8, 24, 101
Edinburgh, Duchess of   101
Edouin, Willy   169, 170, 174, 187
Edward, Prince of Wales (later King
      Edward VII)   7, 24, 40, 47-8, 52, 101

Edwardes, George   xi, xiii, 30, 41, 54. *At
      the Gaiety*   63-70, 72-8, 80, 106, 114,
      117-8, 122-4. *At Daly's*   126-30, 161-
      3, 175-80, 186, 193, 196-9, 203, 208
Elgar, Sir Edward   165, 212
Elixir of Love, The   25
Ellis, Vivian   213
Era, The   159
Everard, Harriet   28-9, 34, 42
Evett, Robert   152, 154, 158, 199

Farren, Nellie   13, 14, 65, 67, 72-3, 105,
      158
Finck, Herman   212
Foli, Signor   173
Forbes Robertson, Sir J.   154
Fraser-Simson, Harold   199
Frear, Louis,   184-6
Fun   17

Gaiety Quartette   65
Gaiety Years, The   xi
George V, King   203
George, John   xii
Gerald Road Police Station   8
German, Sir Edward   xi, xii, 147, 150-8,
      163-8, 200, 210-2, 214
German, Mrs. Winifred   xii, 159, 168
German Reed, Thomas   3-5, 10, 18
Gilbert, Sir William S.   xi, 5-6, 10, 12-6,
      18-21, 23, 25-9, 31-6, 38, 41-5, 47-8,
      52-8, 63-5, 70-3, 77-8, 80-6, 88-90,
      Quarrel with Carte and Sullivan   92-
      8, 100-6, 110-3, 115-6, 123, 125-6, 132,
      134-5, 141-3, 151, 155, 165-8, 187, 214
Gilbert and Sullivan   xii, 97, 105, 197
Golden Legend, The   71
Gounod, Charles   100
Graves, George   176, 187
Green Room Club   206
Greenbank, Harry   129, 130, 139, 42, 144,
      161
Greenbank, Mrs. Nettie   140
Greenbank, Percy   159, 161-2, 178, 208-
      10
Greenbank, Phyllis   xiii
Greene, Evie   120, 162, 170, 176
Grove, Sir George   7-9, 53
Grundy, Sidney   107, 110, 111

Hall, Owen   114, 126, 128, 130, 135, 139, 141, 169, 173, 196, 198
Hamilton, Cosmo   176
Harris, Augustus   103
Hay, Ian (General Ian Hay Beith)   207-8
Helmore, Rev. Thomas   6
Henry VIII   154
Henson, Leslie   205
Hicks, Sir Seymour   116
Hill, Maud   205
Hill, Lucille   113
Hobson, Maud   114, 132
Hollingshead, John   13-4, 16, 35, 63-8, 72
Hollins, Redfern   68, 70
Hood, Marion   42, 68, 70
Hood, Captain Basil   142-3, 145, 151, 154-5, 158
Horton, Priscilla (Mrs. German Reed)   3-5, 10, 18
Howard Talbot papers   184, 208
Hughes, Gervase   117, 170
Huntley, G.P.   76, 192-3

In Memoriam   9
Irving, Sir Henry   154, 159
Isaacs, Mr.   63
Isaacs, Clara   108

Jaeger, Louis   113, 146
Japanese village, Knightsbridge   57
Japanese Legation   57
Jay, Isabel   52, 177, 192-3, 196
Jerome, Leonard,   23
Jones, Arthur   xii, 210
Jones, Dorothy   xii
Jones, Rachel   166
Jones, Sidney,   xii, xii, xiv, 114, 126, 128, 129-32, 135-9, 141, 144-6, 177, 190, 200, 210
Jupp, Jimmy   197

Kendal, Madge   18
Kendal, W.H.   18
Kipling, Rudyard   211
Knights, The   190

Lawrence, Mr. Justice   94, 96
Lecocq, Charles   19, 105
Leeds Festival   44, 56, 71
Léhar, Franz   176

Lehmann, Mrs. R.C.   9
Leigh, Gracie   193
Leipzig Conservatoire   6
Lely, Durward   57, 59
Lester, Alfred   176-7, 186-7
Lessing, Madge   128
Lily of Laguna   xii, 212
Lind, Letty   127, 129, 135, 139, 140, 142
Linley, Hannah Mary (Mrs. Sidney Jones)   130-1, 210
Lingarde, Alice   197
Lingarde and Van Biene companies   197
London Fire Brigade   49
Lonsdale, Frederick   177, 194, 199
Lonsdale, Lesley   199
Lost Chord, The   23
Lytton, Sir Henry   xi, 46, 155, 158

Macintire, Miss   101
Mackenzie, Sir Alexander   165, 167, 211-2
Magistrate, The
Manchester Public Library   xii, 169, 214
Mansfield, Richard   154
May, Edna   175-6
Mayor of Antioch, The   44
McIntosh, Nancy   115, 125-6, 132-3, 166-7
Mendelssohn, Felix   7
Mendelsshohn Scholarship   6
Merson, Billy   213
Metzler, George   25
Midsummer Night's Dream, A   26
Millar, Gertie (later Countess of Dudley)   159, 178-9, 180, 205-6
Miskin, Mrs. Dorothy   xii, 122, 206
Monckton, Lionel   xii, xiii, 114, 117-8, 120-3, 139, 144-5, 159, 161-2, 178, 187-90, 200, 204-5, 209, 214
Monckton, Lady   121
Morton, Edward   144
Mozart, Wolfgang Amadeus   100
Munkittrick, Alexander   181-2
Munkittrick, Howard *see* Talbot, Howard

Nelson, Lord   27
Norwich Festival   9
Novello, Ivor   206

Offenbach, Jacques   7, 19-21, 60, 105

Opéra Comique, The Battle of   34-5
Ours   17

Paget, Cecil   xii
Palotta, Grace   120
Pallant, Walter   177
Parry, Sir Hubert   181
Parry, John   4
Passmore, Walter   46, 115, 134, 143,
     152, 154, 158
Pater, Walter   44
Paul, Mrs. Howard   26-7
Payne, Edmund   116, 158, 180, 196
Performing Right Society   209-10
Perola   48
Phipps, C.J.   47
Pine, Hetty (Mrs. Percy Greenbank)   161
Pirandello, Luigi   11
Planquette   19
Pope, W. Macqueen   213
Pounds, Courtice   82, 87, 113, 176, 183,
     187
Pounds, Louie   176
Pounds, Lorna   212
Pounds, Toots   213
Power, George (later Sir George
     Power)   42
Princes, The   52
Private Eye   198
Punch   17, 124, 161, 209

Raquet, Clothilds,   113, 146
Ray, Gabrielle   128
Reeve, Ada   116, 155, 170-1, 173-4, 190-1
Reed, Alfred   11
Richard III   154
Rival Curates, The   43
Rival Poets, The   153
Roberts, Arthur   106, 123
Robertson, Tom   7
Rogan, Colonel Mackenzie   212
Rolyat, Dan   188, 190
Ronalds, Mrs. Fanny   23-4, 52, 146
Ronalds Pierre, 23, 24
Ropes, Arthur *see* Ross, Adrian
Ropes, Patience   xii, 124
Rosa, Carl   20
Rosa, Parepa   20
Ross, Adrian   106, 114, 121, 124, 159,
     177-8, 197, 208, 210

Ross, Mrs. Joy   xii,   206
Rothschild family   206
Royce, Edward   65
Rubens, Paul   xii, xiii, 161, 186, 190-4,
     196, 199, 203, 209-10
Russell, Lilian   97, 107-9
Russell v Carte   102

Savage, Colonel   164
Schubert, Franz   208
Schumann, Robert   7
Scott, Clement   16, 19, 104, 122, 135
Scott, Herbert   152-4
Scott Russell, John   8-9
Scott Russell, Louise   8
Scott Russell, Rachel   8-10, 24
Scott, Sir Walter   98
Shaw, George Bernard   101
Shaw, Captain Massey   49
Sherbroke, Mrs. Dorothy   68
Sims, George R.   53, 142
Six Characters in search of an Author   11
Smythson, Florence   187-8
Smith, W.H.   29
Society   17
Soldiers of the Queen   xii, 212-3
Solomon, Charlie   107
Solomon, Edward   xii, 107-11
Solomon, Jane   108
Spain, Elsie   166
Sporting Life, The   196
S.S. Bothnia   35
St. Michael's, Chester Square   8
Stanley, Mr. (Carte's solicitor)   97, 102
Stephenson, B.C.   68-9
Stetson, American theatre manager   61
Stirling, Antoinette   23
Stoker, Bram   164
Stoker, Mrs. Bram   155
Stratton Eugene   173, 175
Strauss, Johann   200
Stravinsky, Igor   211
Stuart, Leslie   xii, 169-77, 180, 212-4
Stuart, May Leslie   213
Studholme, Marie   176
Sturgess, Julian   98-9, 101
Sullivan, Sir Arthur Seymour   xi, 4-10, 12,
     14, 16, 18-19, 21-9, 30-6, 38, 63-5, 70-
     3, 77-8, 80, 81-6, 88-90, *Quarrel with
     Gilbert*:   92-105, 107, 109, 111-3,

105-6, 125-6, 132, 134-5, 142-3, 145
  Death: 146-7, 151-2, 155, 158, 163,
  168, 183, 200, 214
Sullivan, Barry   17
Sullivan, Frederick   22
Sullivan, Herbert   23, 113, 143, 146-7
Sullivan, Mrs. Maria   6, 38
Sullivan, Thomas   6, 9, 25
Swinburne, Algernon Charles   44

Talbot, Betty   206
Talbot, Howard   xii, 161, 181, 186-90,
  205-9
Talbot, Hugh   38
Tanner, James   106, 114, 130, 159, 178,
  196-7
Taylor, Charles H.   163
Tempest, Marie   70, 78-9, 126-8, 130-1,
  135-6, 139, 141-2, 144-5
Tempest, The   3, 7
Temple, Richard   42, 57, 183
Tennyson, Lord Alfred   52, 71
Terriss, Ellaline (Lady Hicks)   116-20,
  130, 190, 204
Theatres incorporating theatres, opera
  houses, concert halls etc.
  Adelphi   178-80, 205-6
  Albert Hall   71, 85
  Alhambra   110
  Apollo   163, 192
  Aquarium, Westminster   35
  Avenue (later Playhouse)   183
  Bijoux, Paignton   41
  Covent Garden   31
  Crystal Palace   7, 9, 71
  Daly's   xiii, 118, 123, 126-8, 130-2, 135,
    141, 143-5, 159, 161, 176-8, 182, 198-
    9, 204, 208
  Fifth Avenue, New York   35-6, 61
  Gaiety   xii, xiii, 12-15, 19, 63-9, 72-3,
    105-6, 114, 116, 120, 122-4, 126, 130,
    132, 149, 158-9, 161, 172-3, 175-8,
    180, 192, 195-7, 204-5
  Haymarket   3, 18, 21
  Hippodrome   200
  London Palladium   213
  Lyceum   154

  Lyric   80, 104, 120, 126, 169, 173-7, 186,
    209
  Olympic   35
  Opéra Comique   25-6, 28, 31, 41-2, 44,
    46
  Prince of Wales   69-70, 78, 105, 114,
    175, 177, 186, 192-3, 194
  Princes, Manchester   173
  Queens   187
  Royal English Opera House (later the
    Palace)   90, 99, 102-3
  Royalty, Soho   20, 22, 190
  Savoy   xi, xii, 16, 31-2, 46-9, 50-1, 56, 58,
    60, 62, 64, 67-70, 77-8, 80, 83-4, 86-7,
    89, 90-5, 98, 102, 107, 109, 110, 111,
    114, 116, 125-6, 132, 134-5, 153-5,
    165-6, 200
  Shaftsbury   186-7, 190
  St. George's Hall   4
  St. Martin's Hall   3
  Strand   24, 185-6
  Vaudeville   176, 183
  Winter Garden   205
Thompson, Alex   163
Thomson A.M.   187
Toole, J.L.   14, 159
Tosti, Signor   198
Tower of London   81, 84
Tree, Sir Herbert Beerbohm   154, 168, 192
Tree, Maud (Lady Tree)   54
Trelawny, Lady Rosamund   xii
Turner, Lucy (Lady Gilbert)   17, 52
Twelfth Night   193

Uncle Dick's Darling   159

Vaughan, Katie   65
Victoria, Queen   7, 84, 134, 147
Vincent, Ruth   164-5, 182

Wallis, Bertram   177, 196
Westminster, Duke of   206
Wicked World, The   165
Wilton, Marie (Lady Bancroft)   17, 64
Wood, Ethel (Mrs. Adrian Ross)   123
Workman, Charles   166-7
Wright, Huntley   138-9, 142, 144, 162